# Therapeutic Exercises
# for Children:
## Professional Guide

**Robert D. Friedberg**
**Lori E. Crosby**

Professional Resource Press
Sarasota, Florida

Published by
Professional Resource Press
(An imprint of the Professional Resource Exchange, Inc.)
Post Office Box 15560
Sarasota, FL 34277-1560

Printed in the United States of America

Copyright © 2001
by Professional Resource Exchange, Inc.

All rights reserved

The copy editor for this book was Brian Fogarty, the managing editor was Debra Fink, the production coordinator was Laurie Girsch, and the cover was created by Carol Tornatore.

**Library of Congress Cataloging-in-Publication Data**

Friedberg, Robert D., date.
  Therapeutic exercises for children: professional guide / Robert D. Friedberg, Lori E. Crosby.
    p. cm.
  Includes bibliographical references.
  ISBN 1-56887-064-7 (alk. paper)
    1. Children--Mental health. 2. Cognitive therapy for children. 3. Self-esteem in children. 4. Depression in children. 5. Anxiety in children. I. Crosby, Lori E., date. II. Title.

RJ506.D4 F75 2001
618.92|89142--dc21

                                                    00-059253

# Dedications

I dedicate this professional guide to my parents,
Morton and Rachelle, who encourage my scholarship
And to Barbara and Rebecca
Whose light shines through my life.

*Robert D. Friedberg*


For my parents,
For your support, guidance, and love
For teaching me how
To make a difference in the lives of children.

*Lori E. Crosby*

# Acknowledgments

I would like to acknowledge my co-author Dr. Lori Crosby who is a true and trusted colleague. I want to thank the faculty and administration of the Wright State University, School of Professional Psychology in Dayton, Ohio for their support. I also want to acknowledge the many contributions of the trainees who worked in the PANDY Program. Thank you to the children and parents who participated in the PANDY Program for entrusting their care to us. Finally, much gratitude is given to Dr. Larry Ritt, Ms. Debra Fink, and Ms. Laurie Girsch for their editorial insight, support, and encouragement.

*Robert D. Friedberg*

Thanks to my co-author Dr. Robert Friedberg for his patience, understanding, and the endless hours of editing it took to make this project come to life. Thanks to my colleagues, friends, and the students at the Wright State University School of Professional Psychology for their dedication and encouragement. Thanks too, to Dr. Kathleen Burklow for her enthusiasm and support. Special thanks to my sister for always being there and for giving me a push when I needed it. And always, thanks to the creator for all of the blessings.

*Lori E. Crosby*

# Table of Contents

**Chapter 5 - Working With Anxious Children** (continued)

**Chapter 6 - Working With Depressed Children**    61

**Chapter 7 - Using *Therapeutic Exercises for Children*
    With Groups**    75

**Chapter 8 - Working With Parents**    85

# Therapeutic Exercises for Children:
## Professional Guide

**CHAPTER 1**

# Introduction:
# Goals of This Guidebook

There is a proliferation of workbooks containing various and sundry techniques for clinical work. Practicing therapists tend to be a pragmatic group who enjoy acquiring new tools and applying them in their clinical work. Many workbooks present useful skills but fall short by neglecting vicissitudes involved in using the skills. *Therapeutic Exercises for Children* and this user guide present coping techniques but also discuss many clinical issues related to the workbook techniques.

This guidebook to *Therapeutic Exercises for Children* serves several purposes. First, the guide offers direction to therapists adopting the workbook. Specific examples illustrating ways to apply the techniques are explicated. Secondly, the guidebook provides suggestions and recommendations which enable individualized treatment for specific children. Thirdly, the book alerts readers to salient therapeutic issues, possible pitfalls, and methods for managing various difficulties. Fourth, the guidebook steers therapists through knotty areas by providing contraindications and indications for using *Therapeutic Exercises for Children*. Moreover, the guidebook offers recommendations on cultural adaptations and highlights several central issues relevant to childhood anxiety and depression.

The guidebook functions as a robust resource for additional supporting references. Cognitive-behavioral techniques and the theory underlying their applications are briefly summarized. While the guide provides a skeletal description of cognitive-behavioral procedures with children, it is not a comprehensive text on cognitive-behavioral approaches with children. Accordingly, readers are referred to many recommended resources included in the guidebook.

*Therapeutic Exercises for Children* is a cognitive-behaviorally based workbook that includes exercises, activities, thought diaries, and thought testing procedures. The materials are designed for 8- to 11-year-old children who are experiencing symptoms of depression and anxiety. Many of the workbook exercises and activities were created for and developed in the Preventing Anxiety and Depression in Youth (PANDY) Program sponsored by the Wright State University School of Professional Psychology in Dayton, Ohio. The PANDY Program is a cognitive-behaviorally based coping skills program for elementary school children who are at-risk for depression and anxiety. The PANDY Program primarily consists of clinic-based and school-based skill training groups. While the exercises were initially implemented with groups of children, they can nonetheless be easily delivered through individual treatment.

## THEORETICAL FOUNDATIONS

*Therapeutic Exercises for Children* adopts a coping skills approach to intervention. "Coping," Kendall (1992) wrote, "is the ability to experience a less than optimal situation, face it and accept it, and proceed forward with an adaptive response" (p. 236). Accordingly, the guide and the accompanying workbook focus on helping children manage distressing situations, modulate their mood, and access skills that facilitate productive responses. *Therapeutic Exercises for Children* and the PANDY Program are based on cognitive-behavioral therapy (CBT). More specifically, the workbook and manual are based on the model of cognitive therapy espoused by Aaron T. Beck in his many writings (Alford & A. T. Beck, 1997; A. T. Beck, 1976; A. T. Beck, Emery, & Greenberg, 1985; A. T. Beck et al., 1979). Moreover, work by Kendall and his colleagues (Kendall, 1990; Kendall et al., 1992, 1997; Kendall & Treadwell, 1996). Seligman and his colleagues (Jaycox et al., 1994; Seligman et al., 1995), and Silverman and her colleagues (Silverman, Ginsburg, & Kurtines, 1995; Silverman & Kurtines, 1996) have fundamentally shaped the material included in the workbook and manual. Finally, workbooks for children by Kendall (1990) and Vernon (1989, 1998) as well as the outstanding workbook and manual for adults by Greenberger and Padesky (1995) inspired this format.

The cognitive model of psychopathology states that when children are depressed or anxious, there are changes in five important and inter-related areas (A. T. Beck, 1985; Padesky, 1986). Environmental stressors such as peer rejection or moving from one school to another may occur. Physiological, mood, behavioral, and cognitive changes ensue and are connected to each other in such a way that a change in one sphere accordingly changes the other three domains. In cognitive therapy, intervention is directed at the cognitive and behavioral spheres. Since the areas are all causally interrelated, change in the cognitive sphere will influence behavioral, physiological, and affective symptoms.

Effective cognitive therapy is predicated on two crucial therapeutic leitmotifs: collaborative empiricism and guided discovery (A. T. Beck et al., 1979; J. S. Beck, 1995). Collaborative empiricism is characterized by a working relationship marked by active participation on the part of the child. The collaborative nature of the relationship allows children to be active agents in their own treatment. As a collaborator, the child is encouraged to provide direction and feedback to the therapist. Collaboration with the child is enhanced by checking in with the youngster during each phase of the treatment process. The empiricism component reflects the stance that the child's beliefs are hypotheses to be tested via data collection. Accordingly, therapists are advised to eschew the prior notion that the child's beliefs are automatically inaccurate (Alford & A. T. Beck, 1997). Accuracy is determined through collaborative data collection and analysis. By adhering to collaborative empiricism, therapists create a curious, questioning atmosphere where therapists and children are detectives checking out clues to problems and their solutions (Kendall, 1990; Kendall et al., 1992).

Guided discovery fuels the data collection and analysis process. In guided discovery, children build a data base upon which to evaluate their thoughts and feelings. The therapist acts as a coach during the guided discovery process. The elements of guided discovery include empathy, Socratic questioning, thought testing, and behavioral experiments. The goal in guided discovery is creating doubt where there was once certainty of belief (Padesky, 1988). The therapists' main task is creating a curious milieu in therapy rather than refuting beliefs or persuading the child to think what the therapist thinks. The more the therapist stimulates curiosity in the child, the more the child may be willing to experiment and take risks in therapy (Rutter & Friedberg, 1999).

Cognitive-behavioral therapy (CBT) with children is a structured and directive form of treatment (Knell, 1993). Most forms of CBT include agenda setting, eliciting feedback, and homework assignments (J. S. Beck, 1995). We encourage therapists using *Therapeutic Exercises for Children* to diligently adhere to agenda setting, eliciting feedback, and assigning homework. Chapter 4 deals explicitly with these processes.

Cognitive-behavioral therapy with children has a strong experiential emphasis (Knell, 1993; Ronen, 1997). However, many beginning therapists become overly enamored of techniques and neglect the importance of the experiential component. Perhaps, neglecting the experiential component of CBT is the reason so much therapy goes over children's heads. Maintaining an experiential focus makes abstract concepts real for children.

Neglecting cognitive-behavioral therapy's emphasis on experiential treatment can promote intellectualized or educational therapy. While there is a place for pure acquisition of information, the *Therapeutic Exercises for Children* materials are best applied to children's personal experiences. It is important that children learn to apply the coping skills in context of their own stressors and negative affective arousal. Thus, we recommend that therapists teach the skills acquisition *and* coach the children to experientially apply the skills in meaningful here-and-now contexts. Balancing acquisition and application of the skills is emphasized throughout this guidebook and *Therapeutic Exercises for Children*.

*Therapeutic Exercises for Children* is geared toward making therapy more fun for the child. In recent years cognitive-behavioral therapy has become more playful (Eisen & Silverman, 1993; Friedberg, 1996a; Knell, 1993; Silverman, Ginsburg, & Kurtines, 1995; Stark, 1990; Stark et al., 1996). Accordingly, we recommend that therapists who use the workbook present the material in an entertaining, fun, and engaging manner. There are numerous suggestions throughout the workbook and manual for ways to increase the fun quotient in therapy.

We recommend that therapists adopt a modular, gradually progressive stance toward treatment (Freeman, 1998). Each skill set represents a module and ideally each module builds upon previous ones. Therapists can design treatment modules that respect each child's individuality. The chapters on working with anxious and depressed children instantiate a modular approach to treatment.

The cultural adaptations and clinical indications and contraindications chapters guide therapists toward fitting the exercises to individual children's needs. The issues presented in these chapters promote therapeutic flexibility. The chapters on working with depressed and anxious children provide valuable information on the nature of these disorders in children, intervention planning, and managing various clinical issues with these populations. Therapists will find numerous specific suggestions for using the workbook with individual children and children in groups. Finally, the parent* involvement and school-based intervention chapters describe ways to include parents and recommendations for conducting school-based groups using the *Therapeutic Exercises for Children* material.

---

*The terms *parent, mother, father, caretaker,* and *caregiver* are used interchangeably in this book to refer to the child's parents and other responsible caregivers.

# CHAPTER 2

# Indications and Contraindications

## INTRODUCTION

Deliberate considerations of the indications for the *Therapeutic Exercises for Children* material individualize treatment and potentiate treatment success. Clinicians need to consider the child's presenting problem, comorbidity issues, degree of externalizing problems, severity/acuity of problems, chronological age, developmental considerations, family environment, and responsiveness to traditional cognitive-behavioral interventions when using these materials. In this chapter, we will alert therapists to the specific issues within each consideration.

## NATURE OF PRESENTING PROBLEM

The *Therapeutic Exercises for Children* skills tend to work best with children who are experiencing anxiety and depressive states. More specifically, we recommend this material for children who have depressive spectrum disorders such as Major Depression, Dysthymia, Adjustment Disorder with Depressed Mood, and subclinical levels of depression. Additionally, the *Therapeutic Exercises for Children* approach is primarily suited to children with Generalized Anxiety Disorder, social anxieties, adjustment disorders with anxious moods, and subclinical levels of anxiety. The coping skills in *Therapeutic Exercises for Children* are not recommended as primary interventions for externalizing disorders such as Attention-Deficit/Hyperactivity Disorder (ADHD), Conduct Disorders (CD), or other psychological disturbances such as Bipolar Disorder, Obsessive-Compulsive Disorder (OCD), Panic Disorder (PD), Posttraumatic Stress Disorder (PTSD), and so forth. However, therapists might think about the materials as an adjunctive treatment in some cases. If a skill set in the workbook could be applied to the depressive and anxious features of these children's problems, the *Therapeutic Exercises for Children* tools may be integrated into broader treatment packages that are primarily designed to treat these problems.

## COMORBIDITY

Pure and uncomplicated depression and anxiety are relatively rare in childhood (Gotlib & Hammen, 1992). Consideration of comorbidity issues is important in determining treatment appropriateness. It is far more common for anxiety and depression to coexist with each other than with an externalizing disorder (Kovacs & Devlin, 1998). In fact, anxiety is 2 to 3 times more likely to be comorbid with depression than to be comorbid with a conduct disorder (Kovacs & Devlin, 1998). In a study of 8- to 13-year-olds, 41% of the sample had comorbid depression and anxiety (Kovacs et al., 1989). Last et al. (1992) found that 49% of the 5- to 18-year-olds in their study diagnosed with Overanxious Disorder had a comorbid depressive disorder. The high comorbidity between Major Depression and Generalized Anxiety Disorder in children may reflect shared genetic risk (Kovacs & Devlin, 1998).

Children with mixed anxiety and depression are likely to be characterized by more negative cognitions than children with either depression and anxiety alone (Malcarne & Ingram, 1994). Epkins (1996) found that socially anxious children and dysphoric children demonstrated specific cognitive distortions. For example, personalization (e.g., assuming too much self-blame) and overgeneralization (e.g., erroneously making far-reaching conclusions) were more common in anxious children than in depressed children. Selective abstraction (e.g., inaccurately attending to a negative detail while neglecting other information) was more common for the depressed children compared to their socially anxious counterparts. Heberlein, Lonigan, and Kistner (1997) found that negative self-concepts were associated with both anxiety and depression. They commented that physiological tension and hyperarousal were uniquely associated with anxiety whereas inactivity, low excitability, and lack of enthusiasm were specifically associated with depression. Thus, addressing multiple distortions is critical when working with children experiencing both depression and anxiety.

Anxiety disorders are frequently comorbid with one another. Several authors (Beidel, Fink, & S. M. Turner, 1996; Silverman & Kurtines, 1996) concluded that since fear of negative evaluation is a common theme, Generalized Anxiety Disorder, Separation Anxiety, and Social Phobia can be classified as one group. Accordingly, fear of negative evaluation is a common treatment target for all three disorders. Focusing on fear of negative evaluation is a well-disposed therapeutic strategy in these cases.

Externalizing disorders such as conduct disorders, oppositional disorders, attention disorders, and substance abuse disorders may also accompany depression and anxiety (Birmaher et al., 1996; Curry & Murphy, 1995; Kovacs et al., 1997; Perrin & Last, 1997). Last et al. (1996) found that during a 4-year period, children with Attention-Deficit/Hyperactivity Disorder (ADHD) developed anxiety disorders at a rate equivalent to anxious children. Perrin and Last (1997) remarked that because ADHD children had frequent worries about school and friendship, they may be at an increased risk for anxiety disorders.

Curry and Murphy (1995) noted that substance abuse is likely more frequent among youngsters with higher levels of anxiety. Prepubertal depression is also associated with alcohol and drug use in adolescence and it seems to precede the substance abuse by 4.5 years (Birmaher et al., 1996). Not surprisingly, Manassis and Hood (1998) recommended that clinicians need to develop treatment plans that not only address anxious symptoms but commonly occurring depression, externalizing behavior, and parental anxiety as well.

In summary, anxiety and depression frequently accompany each other. Moreover, separation anxiety, generalized anxiety disorder, and social phobia are commonly comorbid. Externalizing disorders such as conduct disturbances, oppositional disorders, attention deficit disorders, and substance abuse disorders also have depressive and anxious features. The data on comorbidity have several clinical implications. Birmaher et al. (1996) noted that comorbidity increases the possibility of recurrent depression, lengthens duration, exacerbates suicide risk, truncates responsiveness to treatment, and increases the utilization rates for mental health services. Therapists must carefully evaluate which aspects of these problems will be intervention targets with the *Therapeutic Exercises for Children* materials. Fear of negative evaluation cuts across several anxiety disorders and represents a core treatment target. Clinical flexibility is necessary in order to address the multiple cognitive distortions which characterize comorbid depression and anxiety. Further, sorting out the mood components associated with an externalizing disorder is essential.

## DEGREE OF EXTERNALIZING PROBLEMS

As the comorbidity literature suggests, childhood depression and anxiety may be accompanied by other externalizing-type disorders such as Attention-Deficit/Hyperactivity Disorder, Oppositional Defiant Disorder (ODD), and Conduct Disorder. Kovacs et al. (1997) reported that a concurrent externalizing disorder lengthens the duration of a dysthymic episode. Children who were diagnosed with a comorbid externalizing disorder had an average length of Dysthymic Disorder of 6 years whereas the length for a Dysthymic Disorder without an externalizing disorder was 3.7 years. This finding led Kovacs and her colleagues to conclude that "chronic depression may be exacerbated by and/or represent a way of coping with negative social reactions that conduct disturbances elicit" (Kovacs et al., 1997, p. 783). Finally, behavior problems may be a component of anxious or depressive states especially in younger children or children who have difficulty verbalizing their thoughts and feelings. Therefore, therapists must evaluate the degree to which externalizing problems contribute to the child's distress.

*Therapeutic Exercises for Children* is not designed as a primary treatment for ADHD, CD, or ODD. Moreover, children who are very angry or aggressive will not likely profit much from the *Therapeutic Exercises for Children* techniques. Clinical experience gained from the PANDY Program suggests these youngsters have more difficulty with these approaches. There is only one *Therapeutic Exercises for Children* skill specifically designed for anger management problems (e.g., *Surf the Angry Sea*). Accordingly, treatment packages specifically designed for angry and aggressive youngsters are indicated (Feindler & Ecton, 1986; Feindler & Guttman, 1994; Goldstein et al., 1987). Several *Therapeutic Exercises for Children* skill sets which facilitate identifying thoughts and feelings as well as the development of self-instructional dialogues can augment these other approaches.

## SEVERITY/ACUITY OF PROBLEMS

*Therapeutic Exercises for Children* is intended for children experiencing mild to moderate distress. Thus, children who are experiencing severe and acute distress are not the most suitable clients. For example, while the *Therapeutic Exercises for Children* skills are helpful for pessimistic children, youngsters who are hopeless and suicidal need other types of intervention. Children who are in severe or acute distress may benefit from the *Therapeutic Exercises for Children* materials after their distress has modulated. The skills could be used to help maintain their level of functioning and preempt subsequent acute episodes.

## CHRONOLOGICAL AGE

*Therapeutic Exercises for Children* is designed for children ages 8 to 11 years old. The language, cartoons, and metaphors are most suitable for these ages. While chronological age is an important consideration, there is considerable variability between children within this age range. In fact, variation within this age is more the rule than the exception. Therefore, clinicians are advised to weigh developmental issues as well as chronological age when considering using the *Therapeutic Exercises for Children* material.

## DEVELOPMENTAL CONSIDERATIONS

*Therapeutic Exercises for Children* emphasizes developmental sensitivity. All the activities, exercises, and worksheets are constructed to make cognitive therapy principles more accessible to children (Friedberg et al., 1999). A problem common to all child psychotherapies is that treatment becomes too abstract and goes over children's heads. Consideration of emotional, cognitive, and linguistic development is required. Therefore, therapists should try to match developmental task demands with children's developmental capacities.

The *Therapeutic Exercises for Children* worksheets are geared to a 3rd-grade reading level. Children who do not read at this level will have difficulty with the material. While the reading difficulty is not an absolute contraindication, therapists must carefully consider children's reading and comprehension level. The *Therapeutic Exercises for Chil-*

*dren* material is heavily reliant on written and oral expression and reading comprehension. Children who do not read at the 3rd-grade level will have a harder time profiting from the exercises and worksheets. Moreover, these exercises may overly frustrate them and further lower an already fragile sense of self-efficacy. In some cases, therapists may consider reading the exercises and text material to the child. However, in our clinical experience, this is a relatively inefficient strategy since the child is unlikely to fully grasp the material.

Children's ability to translate their innermost thoughts and feelings into words is another developmental consideration. Rudimentary levels of emotional, cognitive, and linguistic development are required. Children who have problems putting words to their thoughts and feelings will have difficulty negotiating their way through the skill sets. Conversely, children who readily express their distress through words will have an easier time with the materials. Graduated tasks are especially important for youngsters with expressive difficulties, and more time and effort will be placed on helping these youngsters use their language to modulate their feelings and actions.

Frequently, the behavior problems associated with anxious and depressed children may be a function of their inability to translate their inner experiences into words. Younger children tend to express depression through more behavioral disturbances (oppositionality, somatic complaints) whereas older children tend to demonstrate more classically adult symptoms (Schwartz, Gladstone, & Kaslow, 1998).

Not suprisingly, it is typical to see more impulsivity and conduct problems in younger, depressed children. They have not learned to put words to their thoughts and feelings. Words mediate action and decrease the impulsive behavior. Older elementary school children whose depressive manifestations include behavior problems represent a different problem. These children either may lack capacity to translate their thoughts and feelings into words, lack the opportunities to develop these skills, or lack access to models or reinforcement sources which support expressing thoughts and feelings (Schwartz et al., 1998).

Evaluating the nature of children's expressive difficulties is critical. The alert clinician must use information gained in their analysis to decide how to most appropriately use the *Therapeutic Exercises for Children* materials with these children. If the problem is a skill deficit, graduated task assignments requiring successively increasing verbal skills are indicated. If the child fundamentally lacks the developmental capacity to turn feelings into words, more behavioral tasks which do not place a heavy reliance on verbal skills may be indicated. Finally, if the child has the skills and the capacity to translate thoughts and feelings into words but lives in a familial context that prohibits expression, adjunctive family treatment seems warranted.

## FAMILY FUNCTIONING

Child psychotherapy is always conducted within a family context. Parents and other caregivers hold many reinforcements for children and establish contingencies for these rewards. Therefore, family members need to be involved in any ongoing child psychotherapy. Chapter 8 includes suggestions for enlisting and maintaining parental involvement in the treatment process. Although *Therapeutic Exercises for Children* is not a set of family therapy techniques, therapists who consider the level of family functioning when using the skills, techniques, and exercises are likely to be more effective.

*Therapeutic Exercises for Children* will likely work well as a stand-alone treatment with children whose family functioning is relatively nonproblematic. For example, family systems characterized by violence, sexual victimization, substance abuse, and strident levels of conflict are unlikely to support gains made by the child in individual therapy. Moreover, enmeshed systems where psychological boundaries are blurred or constricted systems where boundaries are too rigidly defined will also truncate children's gains. In short, if the family system problems seem primary, family therapy is indicated. Some *Therapeutic Exercises for Children* techniques may be used as adjunctive treatments to family therapy to help individual children modulate their mood states.

Psychological disturbance in a parent is a major risk factor for anxiety and depression in children (Beardslee & Wheelock, 1994; Bell-Dolan, Last, & Strauss, 1990; Lee & Gotlib, 1989). Accordingly, clinicians are well-advised to address any parental psychological disturbance. In some cases, recommendations for individual treatment for the parent may be warranted. Limit-setting and parental consistency are additional treatment issues. Many parents are inconsistent with their disciplinary strategies. Indeed, parental inconsistency may contribute to the behavior problems associated with some anxious and depressed children (Beardslee & Wheelock, 1994; Manassis & Hood, 1998). Parental inconsistency can sabotage work with *Therapeutic Exercises for Children*. Therefore, therapists are advised to help parents become better contingency managers.

## USE WITH MORE
## TRADITIONAL FORMS OF
## COGNITIVE-BEHAVIORAL THERAPY

Traditional applications of cognitive-behavioral therapy abound and enjoy considerable empirical support. Treatment packages for depressed children (Seligman et al., 1995; Stark et al., 1996) are well-constructed and empirically tested. Additionally, cognitive-behavioral approaches for anxious children (Albano & Barlow, 1996; Albano & DiBartolo, 1997; Beidel & S. M. Turner, 1998; Kendall et al., 1992, 1997; Silverman, Ginsburg, & Kurtines, 1995; Silverman & Kurtines, 1996) are similarly well-established. Based on children's responsiveness to the traditional cognitive-behavioral methods, clinicians may elect to use *Therapeutic Exercises for Children* tools in conjunction with these approaches or in lieu of them.

The *Therapeutic Exercises for Children* materials can effectively augment other treatment packages. Due to theoretical and conceptual similarities, *Therapeutic Exercises for Children* techniques may be combined with most other cognitive-behavioral treatment approaches. For example, the materials in *Therapeutic Exercises for Children* may be easily integrated into the self-control components of specific treatment programs such as Beidel and S. M. Turner's (1998) social effectiveness therapy for social phobia or Silverman and Kurtines' (1996) pragmatic approach to anxiety disorders. Mixing *Therapeutic Exercises for Children* skills into empirically based treatment recipes may expand clinicians' repertoires and foster flexibility. Thus, we strongly recommend attempting to integrate the *Therapeutic Exercises for Children* tools with other treatment options especially when specific, empirically tested treatment approaches for discrete disorders (social phobia, obsessive-compulsive disorder, etc.) exist.

## CONCLUDING REMARKS

Flexible application of workbook exercises is recommended. Mindful consideration of the indications and contraindications promote facile implementation. *Therapeutic Exercises for Children* can be used as a stand-alone treatment or in combination with other treatment strategies. Therapists' choice regarding the proper application of the material is best made after considering the salient issues presented in this chapter.

The *Therapeutic Exercises for Children* materials represent core treatment components for children ages 8 to 11 years old experiencing mild to moderate depression. In these instances, the level of acuity is low and the family functioning is sufficient to support treatment gains. Further, the youngster demonstrates minimal impairment due to problems with anger or aggression. The child who reads at a 3rd-grade level and is relatively able to translate thoughts and feelings into words is a good candidate for the workbook.

*Therapeutic Exercises for Children* can supplement treatment in numerous other instances. Based on therapists' thoughtful selection of skill sets, the exercises and activities may be combined with other treatment packages aimed at specific disorders such as Conduct Disorder, Attention-Deficit/Hyperactivity Disorder, Obsessive-Compulsive Disorder, and Social Phobia. The exercises may be used adjunctively in family therapy. In sum, alert therapists review the exercises, select the ones that seem most appropriate at a particular phase of treatment, and then apply the technique in session.

# CHAPTER 3

# Culturally Responsive Use of *Therapeutic Exercises for Children*

## INTRODUCTION

Cross-cultural research has shown the importance of considering cultural variables in treatment. Cuellar (1998) aptly noted that culture molds symptom presentation, prevalence rates, and help-seeking behavior. Moreover, Pedersen (1994) suggested that treatment effects are enhanced when interventions are culturally sanctioned. According to Dana (1998), psychological knowledge and understanding may be considered either emic or etic. Emic sources reflect culturally specific information whereas etic sources denote universal phenomena which apply across cultural subgroups. However, Dana cogently argued that the generalizability of many etic frames of reference lack sufficient empirical support to warrant confident claims of generalizability. Rather than designing culturally derived treatment modalities or adapting existing methods to become more culturally responsive, many clinicians mistakenly apply an etic approach to treatment. Simply, treatment approaches that are culturally responsive are more likely to be effective.

Evaluating the cultural appropriateness or responsiveness of existing treatment programs is wrought with challenges. Empirical data regarding prevalence and incidence of anxiety and depressive disorders in diverse children are limited. Additionally, many studies do not report data on the ethnic and cultural background of the children participating in the study. Data on treatment effectiveness with children from varied backgrounds are severely truncated (Weisz, Huey, & Weersing, 1998). Moreover, race is commonly equated with culture (Beutler et al., 1996; Cuellar, 1998). "What is particularly needed,"

Cuellar (1998) aptly wrote, "is to identify those ethnocultural variables that serve as a cultural lens, filtering information, and experiences" (p. 82). In this way, the psychological salience of sociocultural variables may be evaluated (Beutler et al., 1996; Cuellar, 1998).

Therapists who dismiss cultural differences often misinterpret presenting behavior and provide inconsistent treatment (Pinderhughes, 1989); yet, many therapists continue to fail to receive training in cross-cultural issues. In this chapter, we will examine some of the similarities and differences between Caucasian children and children of color on measures of depression and anxiety. Additionally, gender differences in anxiety and depression are also noted. We also offer recommendations on possible ways *Therapeutic Exercises for Children* might be adapted to become more culturally responsive.

## ETHNIC AND CULTURAL DIFFERENCES IN ANXIOUS AND DEPRESSED CHILDREN

Examining depression and anxiety in children of color is complicated by several methodological considerations. First, there is a paucity of research on depression and anxiety in elementary school age children of color. Secondly, the extant research is compromised by measurement problems, nondescript reports of cultural backgrounds, and a lack of within-group studies. Additionally, there is considerable within-group variance in each culture. Therefore, individual differences exist within each cultural and ethnic subgroup. Accordingly, the existing knowledge should be interpreted cautiously. This section will provide some findings on African-American, Hispanic-American, Native-American, and Asian-American children.

### African-American Children

There is relatively more research on African-American children with anxiety and depressive disorders than on other multicultural groups of children. Nonetheless, the research is quite equivocal. Some studies reveal symptomatic differences, whereas other studies fail to detect different symptom patterns. However, the equivocal results suggest that clinicians should remain mindful of potential culturally specific symptom patterns.

Several community-based studies suggest some interesting differences in symptom expression. Caucasian children (ages 9-12 years) displayed a more maladaptive attributional style than their African-American counterparts (Thompson et al., 1998). The Caucasian youngsters tended to explain negative outcomes through self-blame as well as pessimism shaped by the view that events are unchangeable, and the negative effects will pervade across all other areas of their life. DeRoos and Allen-Meares (1998) found that items on the Children's Depression Inventory relating to doing things wrong and being fatigued were not reflective of African-American children's experience of depression. Caucasian children reported that items having to do with school and behaving badly were not representative of their depressive experiences. Results further suggested that depression for African-American children may be more associated with low self-worth and isolation. Depression in the Caucasian children, on the other hand, may be more associated with negative mood states and guilt. In a recent study with 100 4th- to 6th-grade African-American youths, Sanders, Merrell, and Cobb (1999) found that albeit statistically nonsignificant, these youngsters endorsed slightly less internalizing symptoms than Caucasian children.

In a relatively large-scale study, D. A. Cole, Martin, et al. (1998) found some intriguing results. In 5th grade, African-American children scored higher on self-report measures of depression and anxiety. Teacher reports showed higher ratings for the African-American children on measures of depression. D. A. Cole, Martin, et al. noted that since there were nonsignificant differences in the older children, ethnic differences in depression and anxiety may also be shaped by age variables. Ethnic differences may emerge at different ages for various children.

Significant differences between African-American and Caucasian youngsters are not demonstrated in most studies with clinically referred youngsters (Nettles & Pleck, 1994). Politano et al. (1986) investigated differences in depression between African-American and Caucasian inpatient children. They found that the African-American children scored higher on behavioral measures reflecting oppositionally whereas the Caucasian children scored higher on affective indices reflecting depression.

Several studies have examined ethnic and racial differences in anxieties and fears. Treadwell, Flannery-Schroeder, and Kendall (1995) found that 8 of the 10 content areas on the Revised Children's Manifest Anxiety Scale (RCMAS; Reynolds & Richmond, 1985) were endorsed similarly by the African-American and Caucasian children. The African-American children were more likely to endorse the anger items on the RCMAS. Beidel, M. W. Turner, and Trager (1994) investigated test anxiety and childhood anxiety disorders in African-American and Caucasian school children. They found no ethnic differences in test anxiety. However, 50% of the Caucasian children and 62% of the African-American children experienced additional anxiety disorders. Beidel et al. (1994) found a very high percentage (70.6%) of the African-American children met criteria for social anxiety.

Neal, Lilly, and Zakis (1993) compared the common fears of African-American and Caucasian children. They found that both groups of children similarly endorsed 8 out of the 11 most common fears. In their exploratory factor analysis, they found that the school fears factor was not present for the African-American children. Finally, gender and race variables shaped children's responses to the item regarding fears of getting their hair cut. Neal et al. (1993) aptly remarked that since most African-American girls do not get their hair cut until high school, it represents a significant and unique event in these youngsters' lives. Moreover, girls who endorsed this fear were also described as quite sensitive to having their hair combed, brushed, or straightened. Neal et al. concluded that these findings compel clinicians and researchers to mindfully consider cultural issues. In a 12-month follow-up study, Neal and Knisley (1995) found that African-American children's fears were more stable over time than their Caucasian counterparts. They hypothesized that "the stability differences may be due in part to African American children's fear context specificity rather than developmental issues" (p. 159).

African-American children reported more worries than their Caucasian or Hispanic counterparts (Silverman, La Greca, & Wasserstein, 1995). These youngsters had significantly more worries about war, personal harm, and family than their cohorts. Silverman, La Greca, and Wasserstein (1995) suggested these patterns of worries suggest contextual specificity.

Last and Perrin (1993) examined anxiety disorders in African-American and Caucasian children finding that both groups experienced similar patterns of disorders. Separation anxiety, overanxious disorder, and phobic disorders were the most common anxiety problems in both groups. The African-American children had a slightly higher lifetime prevalence for PTSD. Raters estimated a greater anxiety severity in the Caucasian group. Caucasian children were more likely to present with school refusal than the African-American youngsters.

Last and Perrin made some interesting conclusions from their data. First, clinicians may underestimate the severity of anxiety disorders in African-American youngsters and instead focus on internalizing symptoms in these children. Secondly, perhaps anxiety disorders manifest themselves less severely in African-American youths and consequently they are less likely to seek treatment. Finally and most alarmingly, perhaps the African-American children experience the symptoms severely and commonly but they are not identified or referred by health care professionals due to a cultural bias toward attending to the externalizing behaviors of these youngsters.

## Hispanic-American Children

Literature on depression and anxiety in Hispanic-American elementary school children is also quite limited. Most of the research we reviewed focused on older children and adolescents. Thus, more research on elementary school children is necessary. In their study of clinically referred children, Hicks et al. (1996) found that in general, anxious Caucasian and Hispanic children were similar on all clinical variables with the exception that the Hispanic youngsters had slightly more separation anxiety. The Hispanic parents rated their children as more anxious than the Caucasian parents rated their youngsters. Ginsburg and Silverman (1996) reported similar findings indicating that Hispanic children were more likely than the Caucasian children to present with separation anxiety disorder. Moreover, the frequency of anxiety disorders were the same for both the Caucasian and Hispanic youngsters. Simple Phobia, Overanxious Disorder, Separation Anxiety Disorder, and Social Phobia were the most common disorders for both groups. Silverman, La Greca, and Wasserstein (1995) studied worries in elementary school children. They found that Hispanic youngsters worried more about health concerns than the Caucasian children. Further, Hispanic girls worried more about school and performance than Hispanic boys.

## Native-American Children

The research on anxiety and depression in elementary school Native-American children is extremely limited. A literature review revealed several unpublished doctoral dissertations and a few published articles. Clearly, more attention needs to be directed toward understanding internalizing disorders in Native-American elementary school children.

Dion, Gotowiec, and Beiser (1998) studied depression and conduct disorder in Canadian native and nonnative children. They found that the nonnative children rated themselves higher on measures of depression than the Native-Canadian youths. Nonnative parents rated their children higher in depression than the Native-Canadian parents. However, teachers evaluated Native-Canadian children as more depressed than their counterparts.

Dion et al. offered several compelling conclusions that may be applicable to clinicians working with Native-American children. First, there may have been a systematic bias in the teachers' reports of Native-Canadian children's behavior. Dion et al. (1998) remarked, "Cultural misunderstandings may prompt Non-Native teachers to attribute their difficulties with Native children to psychopathology in the latter" (p. 742). Secondly, native children and their parents may be underreporting their depressive symptoms. Thus, mental health professionals need to be alert to the possibility of both the underestimation and overestimation of symptoms in populations of children from nonmajority cultures.

A potential hypothesis for the lack of research in this area may be the nonapplicability of depression and anxiety as operationalized by Western diagnostic classification systems to Native-American children (Allen, 1998). Allen noted several indigenously defined illnesses that may resemble depression such as worry sickness (wan tu tu ya/wu ni wu), unhappiness (ka ha la yi), heartbroken (uu numg mo kiw ta), and disappointment (qo vis ti). These syndromes may resemble depression yet go undetected by traditional measures. Consequently, variations in symptom expression may not appear.

Although the research is unclear and underdeveloped, there is reason to suspect Native-American children suffer from depressive spectrum and anxiety disorders. Suicide is the second leading cause of death in Native-American teenagers (Ho, 1992; LaFramboise & Low, 1998). Further, alcohol and drug abuse is a fundamental problem for Native-American youngsters (Ho, 1992; LaFramboise & Low, 1998). It makes conceptual sense that anxiety and depression may in some way be implicated in the high rates of substance use and suicide in these young people.

**Asian-American Children**

There are few studies examining depression and anxiety in Asian-American elementary school children (Ho, 1992; Huang, 1998; Huang & Ying, 1998; Nagata, 1998). Most of the studies we found investigated psychological problems in older children and adolescents. In explaining the paucity of research, Nagata (1998) stated that Japanese-

Americans are underrepresented in epidemiological statistics and research because they rarely seek mental health services. However, Nagata noted that the lack of data does not necessarily denote the absence of psychological problems.

Citing a study completed in Los Angeles County, Nagata (1998) noted affective disorders were a common diagnosis for Japanese-American youth. Moreover, Japanese-American youth tended to report lower self-concept, especially regarding physical characteristics, than their Caucasian counterparts (Arkoff & Weaver, 1966 as cited by Nagata, 1998). Vietnamese refugee children who left their homeland without their parents experienced pervasive sadness and hopelessness (Harding & Looney, 1977 as cited by Huang, 1998). Finally, Ho (1992) commented that children of Asian immigrants tend to internalize psychological distress contributing to a high number of somatic complaints in these youngsters. For these youngsters, physical complaints may be more culturally acceptable. Since disclosure and emotional expression are possibly discouraged, the physical complaints are expressions of internalized distressed (Ho, 1992).

## GENDER DIFFERENCES

A comprehensive understanding of childhood depression and anxiety requires an appreciation of gender differences. Gender differences are often age-specific and ethnically specific in childhood. Hops (1995) wrote, "Pathways from childhood to adolescence and adult psychopathology are age and gender specific and that these differences may be the result of different social contexts that nurture the development of health or psychopathology for female and male individuals" (p. 428).

Overall, the prevalence rates for depression are similar for prepubertal boys and girls (Nolen-Hoeksema & Girgus, 1995; Speier et al., 1995). However, between the ages of 12 to 15 years old, girls begin to show higher rates of depression than boys and these differences continue into adulthood. Moreover, there are gender and age-mediated differences in children's explanatory styles (Nolen-Hoeksema & Girgus, 1995). Prepubertal girls tend to be more optimistic than their prepubescent male counterparts. Both boys and girls become more pessimistic in early adolescence, but boys tend to become more optimistic than girls by late adolescence. Thus, over time from prepubescence to adolescence, girls tend to become more depressed and pessimistic in their explanatory styles than boys.

Nolen-Hoeksema and Girgus (1995) offered several hypotheses for this trend. First, over time the expectations and evaluations of significant others in young people's lives become more gender biased. People may expect radically different performance competencies for boys and girls. Parents and teachers may unwittingly shape boys' achievement strivings and girls' efforts toward affiliation. Secondly, explanations of similar performances for both boys and girls may become more gender biased. For instance, good and poor performance may be attributed to gender stereotypes (e.g., boys are good at _____, girls are good at _____). Nolen-Hoeksema and Girgus (1995) rightly noted that gender bias is more likely in situations where performance criteria are more ambiguous and subjective. Indeed, high school, college, and work environments are characterized by increasingly subjective performance appraisals. Girls are beginning to compete with boys in more highly valued arenas. The number of equal opportunities for girls decreases with age. As opportunities become more competitive, highly valued, and limited, there is greater potential for gender bias to occur. The hormonal and physical changes which accompany puberty contribute to girls' increasing risk for depression in adolescence. In general, girls dislike the change puberty brings and see their bodily changes as moving away from the body ideal. Nolen-Hoeksema and Girgus commented that body dissatisfaction is highly correlated with depression in girls. Finally, all of the preceding circumstances occur during adolescence when girls' identity is being formed. Nolen-Hoeksema and Girgus concluded that nascent self-esteem is likely to be jeopardized during identity formation.

Several studies have examined gender differences in anxieties and worries. Silverman, La Greca, and Wasserstein (1995) found that girls had more worries about school, classmates, future events, and appearances than boys. Dadds et al. (1997) found that teachers were more likely to nominate boys who demonstrated anxious symptoms than girls who experienced anxious symptoms. Dadds and his colleagues offered some intriguing interpretations of these differences. They hypothesized that teachers may see anxiety as being more problematic in boys than in girls. Secondly, boys may have manifested more disruptive symptoms accompanying their anxiety than girls' symptoms. The disruptive nature of boys' anxious presentation may have elicited greater teacher attention. Finally, Dadds and his colleagues noted that teachers may simply be more attentive to boys than girls in their classrooms.

In community studies, anxious and fearful girls outnumber boys (Beidel & S. M. Turner, 1998). However, in clinic-based studies there are no significant differences between boys and girls in anxiety disorders (Treadwell et al., 1995). Treadwell et al. noted, "Preliminary investigations indicated that at least when anxious symptomatology reaches clinical significance, no gender differences exist in frequency of occurrence" (p. 374). A possible explanation for girls reporting more anxious symptoms in nonclinical situations may be that girls are socialized to be more emotionally expressive. Additionally, it may be more permissible for girls to be fearful and thus, there is higher parental and teacher tolerance for anxious symptoms in girls. Simply, perhaps it takes more for a girl to be referred for anxiety treatment than boys.

## CULTURALLY RESPONSIVE ADAPTATIONS

When working with diverse groups of children, we encourage therapists to make culturally responsive adaptations to the *Therapeutic Exercises for Children* materials. In their review of child psychotherapy outcome, Weisz et al. (1998) lamented the lack of attention to cultural vicissitudes. They argued that extant treatment methods do not generally consider variables such as language, values, customs, childrearing patterns, stressors, and resources embedded within cultural subgroups. Moreover, commenting on the effectiveness of cognitive-behavioral therapy with depressed children, Kaslow and Thompson (1998) remarked, "Little attention was paid to the cultural relevance of the materials used, the intervention strategies incorporated, and the cultural background and sensitivity of therapists who administer the protocols" (p. 154). Thus, while "the underlying assumptions of cognitive-behavioral interventions appear to apply to a wide variety of 9-13 year olds," modifications to the traditional theory practice are indicated (Treadwell et al., 1995, pp. 381-382). Certainly, all children will not respond identically to *Therapeutic Exercises for Children*. Since most of the techniques in *Therapeutic Exercises for Children* were developed when working with predominantly Caucasian children and the effectiveness of cognitive-behavioral treatment has been studied mainly in these same populations, differential responses and reactions by diverse children are quite possible. Accordingly, this section offers several recommendations to increase the cultural responsiveness of the *Therapeutic Exercises for Children* materials.

Like Koss-Chioino and Vargas (1992), we elect to use the term "culturally responsive" as it implies a more active therapeutic stance.

Cultural responsive adaptations need to be considered to accommodate cultural content and cultural context. As defined by Koss-Chioino and Vargas (1992), cultural content reflects "the specific meaning through which social phenomena are constructed, deconstructed, and reconstructed" (p. 7). Accordingly, children's thoughts, feelings, behavioral response styles, and interactional patterns denote cultural content. Thus, responses to the *Therapeutic Exercises for Children* materials may reflect varying cultural content. Additionally, children's responses or reactions to *Therapeutic Exercises for Children* will reflect cultural context. Koss-Chioino and Vargas (1992) wrote, "Cultural context refers to social environments such as family, school, and community and their patterns of interpersonal relationships which affect behavior and cognition in many spheres including therapy itself and the clinical setting in which the therapy takes place" (p. 7). Cultural responsive adaptations should consider content and contextual vicissitudes. Accordingly, issues such as perceptions of therapy, language, and tailoring treatment to individual children will be addressed.

**Understanding Therapy**

Psychotherapy is an unfamiliar notion to most children. Perhaps, this unfamiliarity is especially salient for children with diverse ethnic and cultural backgrounds (Koss-Chioino & Vargas, 1992). Therefore, demystifying therapy for children and their families is an important part of any treatment package. Cognitive-behavioral therapy in general and the *Therapeutic Exercises for Children* materials in particular are well-suited to the demystification process. In fact, introduction to the treatment approach is an explicit part of cognitive therapy (A. T. Beck et al., 1979; J. S. Beck, 1995; Padesky, 1988). By explicitly introducing treatment, agenda setting, and eliciting feedback, therapists not only openly discuss the parameters of therapy, but also actively engage clients in the process.

*Therapeutic Exercises for Children* includes several exercises and activities designed to introduce the treatment model. *Diamond Connections* explicates the relevant dimensions tapped by the *Therapeutic Exercises for Children* materials. Collaborative empiricism and guided discovery directs therapists to omit any inappropriate dimension, add any appropriate one, or elaborate on an underdeveloped aspect of these exercises so a child's cultural context and content may be more completely addressed. Finally, most of the exercises include a *Tips for Children* section which is designed to introduce the task. As outlined in

Chapters 4 to 6, therapists are directed to repeatedly check in with the child as to ensure their understanding and make any adaptations to the material which will enhance the individual child's acquisition and application of the skills.

## Language

Certainly, cultural content and context will influence children's language. Language will clearly mediate children's responsiveness to *Therapeutic Exercises for Children*. Therapists need to be mindful of language barriers which might truncate the effectiveness of the *Therapeutic Exercises for Children* materials.

*Therapeutic Exercises for Children* rely heavily on children's verbal and written expressive and receptive language skills. Although the materials make plentiful use of metaphors and symbols which can modulate language barriers, the metaphors, symbols, and language may create unnecessary obstacles to effective treatment. For instance, for some children the surfing metaphor used in *Surf the Angry Sea* may be unfamiliar and inappropriate. In these circumstances, therapists are urged to develop different metaphors which more fully appreciate the child's experiences. The child and family may be able to offer more robust symbols which may replace the ones provided on the worksheets.

The skill labels used in each worksheet might also neglect cultural variations in some circumstances. For example, *Changing Your Tune, Thought Digger, Breaking the Crystal Ball,* and so on may lack meaning or significance to some children and their families. Adhering to collaborative empiricism and guided discovery will facilitate flexibility in these cases. The skill set labels are not commandments indelibly written in stone. Rather, they are broad guidelines. Therapists, children, and their families are free to make any changes in skill labels and wording that will enhance the workbook's broad applicability.

Finally, examples given on worksheets and exercises should be considered broad rather than narrow exemplars. The examples are designed to illustrate the process of acquiring and applying the skill rather than emphasizing any particular content. Therapists must remember the tenets of guided discovery first defined in Chapter 1 and further explicated in Chapter 4. The goal of cognitive-behavioral therapy in general and for *Therapeutic Exercises for Children* in particular is not to teach children what to think, but rather to help children acquire and apply a wide variety of skills which will help them explain and respond to the various stressors they face.

## Tailoring Exercises to Specific Circumstances

*Therapeutic Exercises for Children* includes a set of general activities and exercises. Each exercise will need to be adapted to the individual children's needs. This is likely to be particularly critical when working with diverse populations. Poverty, oppression, marginalization, and institutional sexism and racism mark the lives of far too many children (Sanders et al., 1999). The *Therapeutic Exercises for Children* materials are flexible enough for deliberate and mindful modification which are responsive to distinctive stressors. More specifically, adaptations which address unique environmental stressors and varying symptom presentations are merited.

A potential strength of *Therapeutic Exercises for Children* is its encouragement of children to report their real life situations. The skills are then applied to particular problems children face. In this way, the tasks are individualized. For instance, an African-American child may complete the *Catching Feelings and Thoughts* diary and report that he felt worried about a salesclerk following him around the store. A young girl may report being sad because she was excluded from an activity because she was a girl. Alert therapists could then seamlessly incorporate these particular stressors into the *Therapeutic Exercises for Children* techniques. These children might be invited to capture their thoughts and feelings about these distressing events and, if indicated, develop appropriate problem-solving strategies.

*Therapeutic Exercises for Children* may also be adapted to accommodate differences in symptom expression. For instance, for a child who manifests their depressive and anxious symptoms through predominantly somatic or bodily complaints, a column could be added on the *My Mouse Traps Worksheet* entitled "Things I feel in my body that trap me." Additionally, the child could indicate its somatic complaints on the *PANDY Coloring Sheets*. For instance, the child could draw a feeling face on PANDY and then color in places in their body where they experience sadness, worry, anger, and so forth.

Attending to anger management issues is another salient consideration. Clinicians are well-advised to evaluate whether the anger is a primary or secondary emotion for youngsters (Leve, 1995). For instance, an anxious or depressed youngster may engage in angry, aggressive behavior for a variety of reasons. Anger and aggressive behavior disturbances may be related to children's sense of helplessness or powerlessness. They act out aggressively to restore control and competence. Consequently, their perceived sense of helplessness may become attenuated. In this instance, aggressive behavior may be a compensatory strategy and a secondary emotion. These children will need to be taught coping skills to manage the primary emotion (e.g., anxiety, depression) as well as behavioral alternatives to aggressive behavior.

As previously mentioned in Chapter 2, *Therapeutic Exercises for Children* is well-suited to children whose primary problems involve anxiety and depression. *Surf the Angry Sea* is the only exercise primarily designed for anger management. However, *Diamond Connections, My Mouse Traps* and *PANDY Fix-It, Changing Your Tune, Catching Feelings and Thoughts, Permanent or Temporary,* and *Thought Digger* may be applied to help children negotiate their way through angry feelings. For children whose primary concern is anger management, *Therapeutic Exercises for Children* will need to be augmented or replaced with other strategies. Yung and Hammond (1995) have developed a culturally responsive anger management program for African-American youths. Seminal work by Feindler and Ecton (1986) as well as Goldstein et al. (1987) are excellent resources for therapists.

The *Therapeutic Exercises for Children* materials may be adapted to accommodate the different roles of the family. Examples on worksheets may be changed to better accommodate varying worldviews regarding independence and dependence. In this way, the sample worksheets become better models. Further, depending on the circumstance, parents, extended family, or other caretakers may be included in the exercises and activities. When working with individual children, we often include family in the exercises and activities. For example, various family members may complete a *Catching Feelings and Thoughts* diary. In this way, consensual beliefs shared by multiple members may be identified and understood. Further, divergent beliefs within the family system may also be similarly identified and understood.

## CONCLUSION

The goal of cognitive-behavioral therapy is providing symptom relief while simultaneously honoring children's ethnocultural context (LaFramboise & Low, 1998). Therapeutic efforts should focus on increasing coping skills and psychological adaptation rather than replacing or extinguishing children's traditional ethnocultural practices (LaFramboise & Low, 1998; Ramirez, 1998). Accordingly, this chapter supplies information on anxious and depressive symptomatology in diverse children. Further, recommendations for culturally responsive adaptations of the *Therapeutic Exercises for Children* skills were suggested.

Adopting a rigid approach to the workbook and coping skills is strongly discouraged. Rather, therapists are encouraged to take an active and flexible stance toward the materials. All the exercises and activities should be tailored to the individual children in order to account for unique environmental, intrapersonal, and interpersonal stressors that diverse populations confront. Therapists are invited to make any changes in the materials that an individual child's circumstance warrants. Changing words, altering examples, modifying metaphors, and elaborating on the exercises' foci are all encouraged in order to match the materials with the child's needs.

# CHAPTER 4

# Working With
# Individual Children

## INTRODUCTION

Many therapists will elect to use *Therapeutic Exercises for Children* in individual therapy. This chapter offers recommendations which enhance the therapist's work with *Therapeutic Exercises for Children.* The chapter focuses on reminding therapists about the salient aspects of cognitive therapy with children, seamlessly integrating exercises into treatment, maintaining a productive balance between therapeutic structure as well as process, adopting a graduated approach to treatment, emphasizing skill acquisition and application, utilizing the exercises to enliven therapy sessions, and reinforcing the importance of putting material down on paper.

## REMAINING MINDFUL OF
## COGNITIVE-BEHAVIORAL TENETS

### Collaborative Empiricism and Guided Discovery

Collaborative empiricism and guided discovery are core therapeutic stances that permeate cognitive therapists' work (A. T. Beck et al., 1979). Collaborative empiricism and guided discovery were briefly defined and discussed in Chapter 1. These two therapeutic stance variables cut across all aspects of therapeutic work with children. Therapists' technical proficiency with the skills included in the workbook will be diluted if collaborative empiricism and guided discovery are neglected. Thus, regardless of the *Therapeutic Exercises for Children* technique chosen, therapists are well-advised to adhere to collaborative empiricism and guided discovery.

Achieving a collaborative stance with individual children has several advantages. Since children are in control of so few routines in their life, collaborating on the nature of therapy is quite empowering. Enlisting children's partnership in the process diminishes the likelihood of oppositional, recalcitrant behavior. Collaborative empiricism communicates the attitude of, "We're in this together" to the child. Moreover, it dethrones the therapist from an omniscient, omnipotent position and makes the therapist seem more like a coach or guide.

While most therapists readily adopt the notion of collaborative empiricism in principle, being collaborative in practice is not an easy task. Therapists are well-advised to holster the urge toward pedagogy and psychological interpretation. We recommend therapists maintain a curious, open-minded, and objective stance toward the data children and families bring to therapy.

A curious stance facilitates children's exploration of their thoughts and feelings. Additionally, creating a "curious" therapeutic milieu fosters children's innovation in action and thought. Clinicians should remain mindful that the initial purpose of guided discovery is casting doubt where there was once certainty of belief (Padesky, 1988). Guided discovery provides an opportunity for children and therapists to form hypotheses, gather data, ask themselves better questions about the data, and make accurate, functional conclusions. Children's degree of belief may vary dimensionally on a continuum from total conviction to complete disbelief. When children are distressed, they believe their negative automatic thoughts strongly. A therapist's first job is shifting children's thinking set from a point of relative certainty to a point of relative skepticism.

Clinical and training experience suggests that when therapists see their role as simply trying to create doubt, they try to get children to "think something else" less often. Consequently, they are not as invested in the children thinking one thing or another. Children profit from this experience in several ways. First, they may not experience pernicious pressures to perform by giving therapists what they want to hear. Secondly, since there is really not a correct answer, children may perceive the situation as less threatening and subsequently become less reactant or oppositional. Finally, when the children feel less pressured, they may become more able to think flexibly and develop alternative responses.

A confabulated transcript* which illustrates the process of guided discovery and collaborative empiricism is presented below. The example amplifies the manner in which therapists might enlist children's involvement in therapy.

*Therapist:* So when you feel worried around other kids, you wonder if they think you are weird.

*Alex:* Yeah.

*Therapist:* I can see how difficult being around other kids would be then.

*Alex:* It's really hard.

*Therapist:* Hmm. . . . Do you think it would be a good idea to check out whether other kids think you are weird?

*Alex:* I don't know. I am not sure I want to check that out. Why would I want to?

*Therapist:* That's a great question. I don't know either. Let's see if we can figure it out together. What might be some good reasons for seeing whether your guess about what kids are thinking about you is correct?

The preceding transcript highlights several important points. First, the therapist did not discount the child's objections to the therapeutic task. Secondly, the therapist crafted the task in a nonprescriptive manner. Rather than assigning the task to the child, the therapist promoted collaboration by enlisting the child's consent to test the belief. Lastly, by asking the child to come up with advantages for evaluating the belief, greater investment in therapy was facilitated.

**Session Structure**

As previously mentioned, cognitive therapy is characterized by a particular session structure punctuated by agenda setting, eliciting feedback, and homework assignments (J. S. Beck, 1995; Freeman et al., 1990). We agree that the trademark session structure should be followed unless there are clear contraindications against its use (Alford & A. T. Beck, 1997). Faithfully following a consistent session structure can prevent therapists' collusion with clients' pathological interaction styles (Persons, 1989). Readers who are interested in more detailed information on session structure are referred to works by A. T.

---

*Names and identifying information have been disguised throughout this book to protect confidentiality.

Beck et al. (1979), J. S. Beck (1995), and Freeman et al. (1990). This section will briefly describe ways therapists may embed *Therapeutic Exercises for Children* within traditional session structure.

Agenda setting with an individual child is a custom which keeps therapy on track while simultaneously honoring the child's particular experiences. Agenda setting is an opportunity for placing items on the table for therapeutic processing. Many cognitive-behavioral texts acknowledge the benefits gained through agenda setting (A. T. Beck et al., 1979; J. S. Beck, 1995; D. D. Burns, 1980, 1989; Freeman & Dattilio, 1992). First, agenda setting helps the child and the therapist agree on the therapeutic wavelength. Each partner in the therapeutic enterprise knows which topics are on the table. Secondly, agenda setting encourages active participation and engagement in therapy. Thirdly, Freeman and Dattilio (1992) rightly contend that agenda setting can help manage and allocate time within the session. Some clients often make hand-on-the-door comments as they leave the office at the end of the session. While these behaviors may not be totally eliminated, agenda setting can decrease the frequency of hand-on-the-door comments.

The following transcript illustrates how a therapist can enlist collaboration on agenda items.

*Therapist:* What would you like to talk about today?
*Dana:* I dunno.
*Therapist:* Well, your Mom tells me that you have been crying every morning before you go to school. Is that something you would want to talk about?
*Dana:* No and it's not *every* morning!
*Therapist:* So you disagree with Mom.
*Dana:* I guess so.
*Therapist:* Hmm. How might it be helpful to you if we talked about what happens in the morning before school?
*Dana:* I dunno.
*Therapist:* Are mornings a fun time or not so fun time?
*Dana:* Not so fun. They stink.
*Therapist:* Sounds really awful. Do you like it when things are awful and stink in the morning?
*Dana:* What do you think? Of course not!
*Therapist:* Maybe together we can figure out a way to make the mornings better. How does that sound?
*Dana:* Okay, I guess.

*Therapist:* Alright then. Let's begin to figure this stuff out. I'm going to count on you to tell me what mornings are like.

The therapist works assiduously in engaging an initially reluctant child. Secondly, the transcript amplifies the way agenda setting potently endows the child with responsibility. Thirdly, the therapist clearly communicates that the child and therapist form a team which will tackle the child's problem.

## Eliciting Feedback

As mentioned in Chapter 1, eliciting feedback is an important corollary to agenda setting. The chance to give feedback to an adult in authority is a very heady experience for a child. Further, the act of simply being asked for feedback engages the child in therapy. This section will provide therapists with some guidelines for eliciting and processing feedback from individual children.

Classic cognitive therapy texts fully explain the feedback process (A. T. Beck et al., 1979; J. S. Beck, 1995; Freeman et al., 1990). Accordingly, readers are referred to these sources for more in-depth coverage. However, we will delineate several general guidelines for eliciting feedback. Therapists should avoid asking questions such as "What did you like about today's session?" Many children will not be forthcoming with things they dislike. Rather, we suggest therapists ask questions such as:

- What was helpful about today's session?
- What was not helpful?
- What thoughts and feelings about our work today would you like to share?
- What bugged you about today's work?
- What just didn't seem right for you?

Not surprisingly, some children are reluctant to give feedback. Often, the children's reluctance provides yet another look into their inner worlds. Some children fear disappointing or upsetting the therapist. Others may be overly obedient and facile people pleasers. Still other youngsters may hold cultural prohibitions about giving feedback to adults. Some children may be characteristically passive and withholding. Regardless of the individual beliefs and motivations behind their reluctance to give feedback, therapists should process the difficulty giving feedback. Questions such as "What don't you enjoy about giving feedback," "What is hard about giving feedback," and "What are you afraid will happen if you give feedback" are fruitful questions.

**Homework**

Homework is an essential part of cognitive therapy (J. S. Beck, 1995; Greenberger & Padesky, 1995). Accordingly, we strongly recommend homework assignments based on the *Therapeutic Exercises for Children* skills. "Mousework" connotes homework in *Therapeutic Exercises for Children*. Mousework allows children to practice skills outside of the therapy session. These assignments promote generalization by giving children opportunities to gain mastery experiences. Moreover, mousework reflects cognitive-behavioral therapists' emphasis on helping solve problems in the contexts in which they naturally occur (Spiegler & Guevremont, 1995). Further, mousework enables children to figuratively take the therapist home with them. In this way, mousework is a practical and impactful "transitional object." Finally, mousework assignments serve an ongoing assessment function. Simply, therapists can easily see what aspects of therapy are working and which parts are not working. Mousework assignments also provide information on which salient psychological or situational issues are on target.

Mousework should be clearly connected to children's presenting complaints. The closer the association between the exercise and the children's problems, the more psychologically meaningful the assignment will be. Therapists are encouraged to give specific instructions regarding mousework assignments. Many *Therapeutic Exercises for Children* tools contain rather extensive instructions and guidelines to children. However, children need to clearly know when and what parts to complete for mousework. Mousework accompanied by specific instructions is less likely to be misunderstood and misapplied.

Small graduated task assignments are preferred over large mousework tasks. We recommend that initially therapists break up mousework assignments into smaller components and help children gradually move toward the completion of larger tasks. For example, the *Catching Feelings and Thoughts* diary includes several components (e.g., identifying problem situations, recording feelings, rating the intensity of feelings, and capturing automatic thoughts). Therapists may elect to have children initially complete the event and feeling columns. Then, once they have mastered these components, they can fill out the remaining columns.

We recommend that therapists remember to begin mousework assignments in session and not leave them until the last moments of a session. Mousework is recorded on the *Memory Jogger* worksheet. Writing down the mousework is another form of practice and it serves as a reminder over the week for the child. When children successfully attempt their mousework, reinforcements should clearly follow. These reinforcements could be verbal (e.g., "You really worked hard on the worksheet"), written notes alongside the mousework or on the memory jogger, stickers pasted along the memory jogger assignment, or tokens that could be redeemed for small prizes. Regardless of the specific reward, therapists should clearly reward children's mousework efforts.

It is critical that therapists follow-up on any mousework assignment. Assigned mousework left unattended or neglected by the therapist facilitates treatment noncompliance. If children attempt the assignment and therapists do not follow-up with the task, children begin to get the message that mousework is unimportant. Consequently, encouraging children to work on their skills becomes more difficult.

## SEAMLESS INTEGRATION OF EXERCISES INTO THERAPY

The *Therapeutic Exercises for Children* skills need to be seamlessly integrated into therapy sessions. Therapists are well-advised to consider how the exercises augment their work with children at difficult or emotionally meaningful times. The exercises should flow naturally from the session content. For instance, if a child has identified catastrophic thoughts and their accompanying anxious feelings, therapists could pull out the *Changing Your Tune, Breaking the Crystal Ball,* or the *Real or False Alarms* diaries. Seamless integration requires therapists to know why they are using the diaries. The intervention planning section in the anxiety and depression chapters are useful templates for therapists seeking seamless integration.

The exercises and activities should not be used as a last resort for frustrated therapists who are fed up with children's nonresponse to treatment. Selection of the specific *Therapeutic Exercises for Children* techniques require deliberation and forethought. Any technique should advance the therapeutic relationship and build therapeutic momentum by promoting symptom change. If therapists apply the *Therapeutic Exercises for Children* workbook out of context, children are less apt to respond well. Further, using *Therapeutic Exercises for Chil-*

*dren* as a way to distance oneself from noncompliant or difficult children likely leads to unproductive therapy.

In sum, the *Therapeutic Exercises for Children* materials are like toys in a child therapist's toy cabinet. Toys and exercises have a purpose and upgrade traditional "talk" therapy. When therapists and children play with puppets, the puppet play is tied to children's presenting problems and therapists work session content into the puppet play. Similarly, the *Therapeutic Exercises for Children* skills should be assimilated into an overall treatment strategy.

## MAINTAINING A BALANCE BETWEEN STRUCTURE AND PROCESS

Most experienced therapists realize therapy is a juggling act where structure, content, and process are in delicate balance (R. D. Friedberg, 1996b). Effective *Therapeutic Exercises for Children* techniques strike a harmony between structure, process, and content. Each exercise and activity has structural, process, and content elements. Maintaining an equilibrium among the three components enlivens individual therapy.

The structural aspects of each *Therapeutic Exercises for Children* activity are relatively straightforward. Simply, the exercises and activities are the things therapists do in therapy (e.g., completing *Diamond Connections, Real or False Alarms* worksheets).They add focus to individual sessions and form a framework for interventions. Therapists build on the foundation the structure provides.

Content is reflected in what the child says or does during the activity. Simply, content is the material elicited in response to the structure. Children's particular thoughts and feelings are the content included in the *Catching Feelings and Thoughts* exercise. Each *Therapeutic Exercises for Children* activity pulls for particular content. Moreover, content will vary for each individual child. Content is one aspect of therapeutic material generated by the exercise's structure and provides personalized information on each child.

Therapeutic process is the second form of material generated by the structure. If content denotes the *what* of the therapy, process symbolizes the *how*. Process is represented in the way children complete tasks or respond to exercises. For instance, an individual child may disclose his or her thoughts and feelings openly in an affectively expressive manner whereas another child may platitudinously complete a worksheet. Process captures these vicissitudes of individual children's responses. Attending to the process of the *Therapeutic Exercises for Children* further individualizes treatment.

Structural aspects are identical for each child whereas the content and process varies. Each child may respond to the exercises differently. By balancing structure, content, and process, therapists provide an active and direct package while honoring each child's individual characteristics. In this way, the techniques in *Therapeutic Exercises for Children* achieve maximum flexibility.

Artful use of *Therapeutic Exercises for Children* makes use of structure, process, and content. For instance, the *Sticks and Stones* worksheet represents a structure which yields therapeutic process and content. Therapists could use the *Sticks and Stones* worksheet to lessen children's tendency to apply overgeneralized negative labels to themselves. The worksheet exercise provides the structure for identifying and modifying these labels.

The actual labels children use denote the particular content. An individual child might say, "I'm fat," "I'm stupid," "I'm ugly," or "I'm a doofus." These statements are the cognitive content the techniques target. The process reflects the child's reaction to doing the exercise and sharing the cognitive content with the therapist (e.g., the child is fearful about disclosing thoughts). Alert therapists make use of structure, process, and content.

The following transcript shows how structure, process, and content can be utilized with the *Sticks and Stones* worksheet.

*Therapist:* (After the child completed the *Sticks and Stones* worksheet) Do you think you have an idea about what sticks and stones labels are? (Structure variable)

*Greg:* I think so.

*Therapist:* What sticks and stones labels do you call yourself? (Content variable)

*Greg:* I dunno.

*Therapist:* How hard is it to share your labels?

*Greg:* A little.

*Therapist:* What makes it hard? (Process variable)

*Greg:* If I say them, it makes them more real and then you know about them, too.

*Therapist:* So it's hard to tell other people about your labels and by saying it, you make it more real.

*Greg:* Pretty much.

*Therapist:* How would it be to test this out? (Process variable)

| | |
|---|---|
| *Greg:* | Test what out? |
| *Therapist:* | Your hunch that if you say it or share it, the label becomes more real. |
| *Greg:* | I guess that would be Okay. |
| *Therapist:* | Great. Let's try writing out the names you call yourself when you feel bad. (Content) |
| *Greg:* | (Writing on paper) I'm a loser. |
| *Therapist:* | How do you feel when that goes through your mind? |
| *Greg:* | Awful. Sad. |
| *Therapist:* | What is it like to write it down on paper? (Process variable) |
| *Greg:* | It really didn't make me feel that bad at all. It was kinda good to get it out of me. |
| *Therapist:* | So that was surprising for you. |
| *Greg:* | Yes. |
| *Therapist:* | Now, remember what we do with these useless sticks and stones labels. We have to throw them in the trash. (Structure variable) |

The transcript illustrates the way therapists integrate process, structure, and content. The therapist moved from one element to another in a coherent fashion. The structure provided a springboard for the content and process. Content and process were woven together in the therapeutic fabric. By attending to content and process, skill acquisition was tailored to the child's individual experiences. General skills were taught and embedded with the child's psychological and interpersonal contexts.

## GRADUATED APPROACH TO TREATMENT

All the worksheets in *Therapeutic Exercises for Children* are based on a graduated approach to treatment. In a graduated approach, therapeutic tasks and goals are broken down into small, definable, successive steps. Treatment is matched to the child's functioning level.

There are several advantages to a graduated approach to treatment. First, graduated tasks promote self-efficacy or the perception that one can capably accomplish goals (Bandura, 1977b, 1986). Graduated tasks create opportunities for mastery, and successful experiences prompt greater self-efficacy perceptions. Bandura (1977a) argued that increased self-efficacy is fundamental to therapeutic change.

Since not all goals promote motivation, Bandura (1977b, 1986) outlined salient properties of effective goals. Graduated tasks communicate a coping philosophy to children. Mastering successive steps toward ultimate progress propels motivation and swells children's burgeoning self-confidence. The task's challenge level should require moderate effort that results in successful performance. Further, specific goals are preferred over vague, abstract goals. Goal specificity directs children's attention to the requisite steps necessary for goal attainment. For instance, a specific goal is "doing three fun things per day for the next week." An abstract goal would be "feeling better about yourself." The specific goal communicates clear expectations and children can readily recognize when they have met the goal. Finally, immediate goals facilitate greater motivation than distant goals planned far into the future. As Bandura aptly argued, short-term daily goals increase mastery and intrinsic interest. Moreover, they focus direction and attention, and provide ongoing rewards.

## SKILL ACQUISITION VERSUS SKILL APPLICATION

Teaching clients skills is a fundamental process in cognitive-behavioral therapy. Acquisition and application phases are complementary components of most self-control, self-instructional, and cognitive-behavioral approaches to psychotherapy (A.T. Beck et al., 1985; Finch, Nelson, & Ott, 1993; Meichenbaum, 1985). Initially, the process generally begins with children acquiring skills and information. The next phase involves children applying their newfound skills to their own distressing problems. In our clinical experience, we have found that acquisition is readily accomplished whereas application is much more difficult.

Application is facilitated by practice. Furthermore, the practice should occur in the context of negative arousal. Simply stated, children should practice their acquired skills in situations that elicit negative feelings (Robins & Hayes, 1993). In our clinical opinion, it is just not enough to practice cognitive-behavioral skills when children are calm. Practice must occur when they are feeling anxious, angry, or depressed. Success is best measured by the child who completes a thought diary when he or she is feeling badly, rather than by the child who completes thought diaries in relatively sanguine mood states.

Application may occur in graduated phases. Homework assignments, exposure trials, and in-session experiments are ways for youngsters to apply their skills. Creating fun and interesting opportunities for children to apply their acquired skills is a necessary therapeutic task. For instance, a shy child may be encouraged to ask a therapist's receptionist to borrow a pencil or pen. This experience could be processed and used as data to disconfirm a child's catastrophic expectations.

The worksheets and activities are ideally used as mini-exposure trials for the children. The therapist first teaches the child the skills embedded in the worksheet and then helps the child implement the tools when they feel badly. Therapists should assiduously avoid using the worksheets as abstract, intellectualized activities. Skill application is best accomplished through experiential learning opportunities.


## EXERCISES AS A WAY
## TO ENLIVEN THERAPY

The materials in *Therapeutic Exercises for Children* are designed to enliven therapy sessions with children. Many of the exercises are fun ways to present psychological concepts and coping skills to children. We encourage therapists to present the material in a stimulating, engaging, and fun manner. If the exercises are presented in a dull way, children are likely to find them boring. Accordingly, this section gives therapists some suggestions to make *Therapeutic Exercises for Children* come alive for youngsters.

Therapists are encouraged to give themselves permission to enjoy the activities with the children. Acting silly and having fun with the activities are recommended. The activities and exercises are starting points rather than endpoints. Therapeutic innovation, creativity, and inventiveness are strongly suggested.

Personalizing and playfully presenting the material add depth to the skills. For instance, merely assigning written tasks to the youngsters is an unidimensional approach. However, creating dramatic and entertaining play scenes which provide children with the opportunity to personalize as well as rehearse the skills adds another dimension to the exercise. In these instances, the workbook progresses from a static one-dimensional tool to a rather depthful three-dimensional instrument for change.

Several examples from our experience training doctoral supervisees in the PANDY Program at the Wright State University School of Professional Psychology amplify these points. When working with the *Surf the Angry Sea* exercise, several energetic trainees demonstrated a "silly surfing" style. In another instance, a particularly creative trainee dressed up like a fortune teller to introduce the *Breaking the Crystal Ball* diary. Therapists can augment the worksheets with fun dramatics. Additionally, therapists might invite children to use different voices for each choice in the *Permanent or Temporary* worksheet. For example, if they selected the Temporary option, they might use a soft whispering voice. If they chose the Permanent option, they could use a loud, booming voice. Finally, to enliven the *Diamond Connections* exercise, several trainees made bases for the children to actually stand on or pass around as they talked about their thoughts, feelings, behaviors, and bodily reactions. Children will likely remember the concepts and skills which are associated with fun activities more than if they are explained in a dry and unentertaining manner.

## IMPORTANCE OF WRITING
## MATERIAL DOWN ON PAPER

Some therapists are quite reluctant to write things down on paper during a session. However, in our experience, jotting down children's products on paper has several advantages. First, when children see their words written down on paper, it communicates that the therapist is listening. Second, reviewing their problems in written form helps youngsters objectify and gain distance from their distress. Third, written assignments provide a concrete record of children's progress. When the therapy work is translated into written form and communicated to the child, the therapy process loses much of its mystery.

Completed exercises and assignments form the foundation for relapse prevention and treatment review. Additionally, when children inevitably reach a stuck point in therapy, pulling out competed exercises for review can often help the child and therapist negotiate the impasse. Concepts can be reviewed and relearned, progress can be reinforced, and the child's sense of self-efficacy can be strengthened.

Finally, therapists should give children a copy of any tips for children and/or sample exercises that they think would be beneficial to them. The tips and samples provide a useful model for the youngsters.

## CONCLUSION

The *Therapeutic Exercises for Children* techniques augment therapists' repertoires. However, the skills are not merely a magic bag of tricks. Graceful application of skills requires appreciating fundamental cognitive-behavioral principles. Preserving a collaborative stance that promotes an empirical approach to clinical work sparks effectiveness. Embedding the skill set in the proper session structure is a critical therapeutic task.

Synthesizing structure, process, and content makes for coherent application of *Therapeutic Exercises for Children*. Adopting a graduated approach to treatment builds self-efficacy and self-confidence. Accordingly, therapists should break down the skills into small components so the youngsters can readily acquire the techniques. Finally, therapists must work diligently to make the exercises come alive for the children. Therapists must personalize the exercises and help the youngsters apply the skills in an engaging manner.

CHAPTER 5

# Working With Anxious Children

## INTRODUCTION

Working with anxious children and their families can be a challenging yet rewarding experience. This chapter specifies guidelines and resources for therapists using *Therapeutic Exercises for Children* with anxious children. The chapter begins with a brief description of the nature of worry, anxiety sensitivity and behavioral inhibition, generalized anxiety, and social anxiety in children. Additionally, the common cognitive features which characterize anxiety in children are delineated. A section on intervention planning utilizing the *Therapeutic Exercises for Children* follows. Finally, the chapter concludes with a discussion of pertinent issues regarding working with anxious children, such as the importance of exposure and multiple treatment considerations.

## WORRIES

Understanding childhood worries is important to treating childhood anxiety. Worrying is a hallmark symptom in Generalized Anxiety Disorder and Separation Anxiety Disorder (Perrin & Last, 1997; Silverman, La Greca, & Wasserstein, 1995). Silverman, La Greca, and Wasserstein (1995) found that increased worry was correlated with higher levels of anxiety. More specifically, highly anxious children suffered a great number of worries and rated those worries more intensely than children who were less anxious. Thus, worry may be an important factor in the initiation, exacerbation, and maintenance of the anxiety disorder (Perrin & Last, 1997).

Worry can be defined as an "anticipatory cognitive process involving repetitive thoughts related to possible threatening outcomes and their potential consequences" (Vasey, Crnic, & Carter, 1994, p. 533). Vasey and his colleagues noted that worry is commonplace in elementary school children (Vasey et al., 1994). In fact, they found that 8- to 9-year-olds and 11- to 12-year-olds had more worries than 5- to 6-year-olds. Thus, worrying becomes more prominent and intense in middle to late grade school years. Moreover, the nature of children's worries changes during the middle school years when youngsters begin to worry less about physical things and more about abstract issues. Beginning at around 8 years old, children start to worry more about personal competence and social evaluation.

Children typically experience these thoughts and images as being intrusive (Silverman, La Greca, & Wasserstein, 1995). Silverman and her colleagues aptly commented that for some children, worrying is a functional process allowing them to ostensibly rehearse reactions to situations they perceive as threatening or uncontrollable. However, for children with anxiety disorders, the worrying is perceived as uncontrollable and has lost its functional or adaptive value. Vasey (1993) noted, "Worry is a distortion of normally adaptive attempts at anticipation and preparation in that the worry process rarely leads to effective solutions" (p. 7).

Excessive worrying ruptures problem-solving efforts in several debilitating ways (Vasey, 1993). Worrying strengthens the perception that one is incompetent. Further, worrying often fuels catastrophic thinking and dire predictions. For youngsters who already have brittle views of their competence, anticipating danger can be overwhelming. Thus, their coping efforts are likely to deteriorate. Not surprisingly, the cognitive, behavioral, and emotional avoidance which accompany worrying compromises flexible problem-solving. Thus, the children's responses become rigidified and the youngsters literally "freeze up" in stressful situations.

## BEHAVIORAL INHIBITION
## AND ANXIETY SENSITIVITY

Behavioral inhibition and anxiety sensitivity are two constructs which shed light on childhood anxiety. Behavioral inhibition is characterized by withdrawal, timidity, and clinginess in novel situations (Bernstein, Borchardt, & Perwien, 1996). Temperamental inhibition lowers children's thresholds for physiological arousal which increases their anxiety sensitivity and makes it difficult to adjust to stressors (Beidel & Morris, 1995). For example, Manassis and Hood (1998) remarked that, "Children who cope poorly with emotional arousal would probably be more vulnerable to anxiety disorders and show greater impairment when they become anxious" (p. 428). Behavioral inhibition is related to irritability in infancy as well as shyness in toddlerhood (Pollock et al., 1995). Pollock et al. suggested that in school-age children, behavioral inhibition is associated with caution, introversion, behavioral restraint, and physiological arousal in unfamiliar situations.

Anxiety sensitivity is a related construct that may also present a risk factor for anxiety disorders. According to Weems et al. (1997), "Anxiety sensitivity is indicated by the belief that anxiety-related sensations such as heart beat awareness, trembling, and derealization have negative social, psychological, or physical consequences" (p. 961). Weems et al. (1998) explained that children with high anxiety sensitivity believe the experience of anxiety itself predicts dreaded consequences such as a heart attack, insanity, or social censure. Becoming anxious is seen as disastrous, and consequently any activity associated with these noxious sensations is avoided. Youngsters with high anxiety sensitivity imbue anxiety with powerful predictive qualities rather than seeing it as simply another emotion. Thus, behavioral inhibition and anxiety sensitivity reflect anxious youngsters' difficulty managing heightened emotional arousal.

Anxiety sensitivity may lower children's self-efficacy (Vasey, 1993). The feelings themselves are seen as dangerous and overwhelming. Consequently, anxiety-sensitive youngsters believe they will have difficulty modulating their troubling feelings. As Vasey (1993) wrote, "In circumstances in which children believe themselves to be incapable of managing their anxiety, it is conceivable that they will become hypervigilant for even very subtle cues that are associated with anxiety and become anxious when they occur" (p. 30). The hypervigilance in turn contributes to greater apprehension and promotes youngsters' pervasive edginess.

## GENERALIZED
## ANXIETY DISORDER

Generalized Anxiety Disorder (GAD) is a particular anxiety disorder that presents in multitudinous ways. GAD subsumed Overanxious Disorder of Childhood (OAD) in the *Diagnostic and Statistical Manual of Mental Disorders* (*DSM-IV*; American Psychiatric Association [APA], 1994). The central, hallmark feature of the disorder is diffuse global worrying rather than worries about specific situations or objects (APA, 1994; T. H. Ollendick & D. G. Ollendick, 1997; Silverman & Ginsburg, 1995, 1998). Frequently, an intense, irrational worry about the future is present (Strauss et al., 1988). Further, children with GAD often worry about performance, health, and trivial events (Silverman & Ginsburg, 1998). T. H. Ollendick and D. G. Ollendick (1997) noted that in order to receive a diagnosis of GAD, the worry must persist for more days than not over a course of 6 months, be experienced as difficult to control, and have at least one other accompanying symptom including restlessness, fatigability, concentration difficulties, irritability, muscle tension, or sleep disturbances.

Klein and Last (1989) identified overconcern with competence and marked self-consciousness as features of GAD. Children with GAD are likely to be emotionally reactive and find it difficult to relax (Eisen & Silverman, 1993; Kronenberger & Meyer, 1996). Not surprisingly, somatic complaints such as headaches, stomachaches, and general malaise in otherwise healthy children are quite common (Callahan, Panichelli-Mindel, & Kendall, 1996; Kronenberger & Meyer, 1996). Further, nail biting, hair pulling or twirling, and knuckle popping are additional behavioral manifestations (Kronenberger & Meyer, 1996).

Children with GAD have many social concerns and worries about fears of negative evaluation by others (Ginsburg, La Greca, & Silverman, 1998). These youngsters are easily embarrassed and dread others' criticism or ridicule which contributes to a pervasively tense manner (Callahan et al., 1996). Anxiety impairs peer relationships and results in painful social withdrawal (Callahan et al., 1996; La Greca, 1997). In fact, Kashani and Orvaschel (1990) noted that "Anxiety exerts its most detrimental effects on the interpersonal spheres of functioning" (p. 318). Children with GAD are often seen as less assertive and outgoing (Ginsburg et al., 1998). This marked self-consciousness contributes to edginess and a sense they are walking on egg shells. Youngsters with GAD report more negative interactions, teasing, and enemies in school (Ginsburg et al., 1998). Not surprisingly, these children may be more comfortable around adults than they are around other children and may present in a pseudomature manner behaving like miniature adults but lacking access to truly mature coping skills (Kronenberger & Meyer, 1996). Not surprisingly, youngsters with GAD rate their social acceptance and global self-worth low (Ginsburg et al., 1998).

Eisen and Silverman (1993) remarked that children with GAD are typically "overachievers with high expectations for competent performance in academic, social, and athletic arenas" (pp. 265-266). These youngsters tend to be highly perfectionistic, constantly seeking excellence, and excessively self-critical when they inevitably fall short of their unrealistic standards. Accordingly, these children are plagued by excessive self-doubts and repeatedly seek reassurance from others to soothe their insecurities (Callahan et al., 1996; Kronenberger & Meyer, 1996). Indeed, anxious children appear caught in a bind where they value achievement but perceive themselves as unable to perform at expected levels.

Costanzo, Miller-Johnson, and Wencel (1995) noted that anxious youngsters tend to lack perceived control and self-efficacy. They aspire for rewards yet believe they cannot complete or consistently execute the responses that bring about desired outcomes. This explains the common circumstance in which highly successful children doubt their competence. In essence, these youngsters hold a helplessness orientation in which they do not see their successes as internally controlled or replicable (Diener & Dweck, 1980). Anxiety truncates children's range of experiences. Bell-Dolan and Wessler (1994) stated that anxious children tend to avoid important stimuli such as peers, extracurricular activities, and school — all of which facilitate healthy adjustment.

## SOCIAL PHOBIA/SOCIAL ANXIETY

Social Phobia replaced Avoidant Disorder of Childhood in *DSM-IV* (APA, 1994). Social phobia truncates children's social functioning. In this condition, children experience so much social or interpersonal discomfort that normal socialization is inhibited. These children are not merely slow to warm-up in social situations, they are so terrified that making friends becomes excruciatingly painful. Typically, socially phobic youngsters are uncomfortable in situations where there are peers who they do not know well or in circumstances where they will be under intense scrutiny (American Academy of Child and Adolescent Psychiatry, 1997).

Kendall et al. (1991) describe social phobia in childhood as "stranger anxiety that continues beyond the developmental timetable" (p. 132). Socially anxious youngsters fear negative evaluation and dread acting in an embarrassing or humiliating manner (American Academy of Child and Adolescent Psychiatry, 1997). Not surprisingly, these feelings may contribute to youngsters freezing up in social or evaluative situations (Silverman & Ginsburg, 1998). Socially phobic youngsters are commonly reluctant to speak in class and rarely attend fun social activities (Beidel & S. M. Turner, 1998). Further, they lack confidence that they can make friends. Indeed, these youngsters "often stand at the perimeter of other children's social activities" (Beidel & S. M. Turner, 1998, p. 37).

In fact, breaking into small groups in class or selecting a partner to work with on a school task is a common anxiety-producing experience for socially anxious children (Beidel & S. M. Turner, 1998). The most common dreaded events socially anxious youngsters fear include unstructured encounters with peers, taking tests, performing in front of others, and reading aloud in front of others (Beidel & S. M. Turner, 1998). Test anxiety may be associated with social phobia (Beidel et al., 1994). Children fear negative evaluation and have many physical symptoms when they anticipate tests or take exams (Beidel & S. M. Turner, 1998).

The age of onset for social phobia is generally from late childhood to early adolescence, with the mean age ranging from 11.3 to 12.3 years old (Beidel & Morris, 1995). However, children as young as 8 years old can experience social phobia (Beidel & S. M. Turner, 1998). Children typically experience physical symptoms including choking, flushing, chills, heart palpitations, fainting, shaking, feeling like dying, and headaches (Beidel & S. M. Turner, 1998). Beidel and S. M. Turner (1998) suggested that it may be more difficult for younger children (ages 8-12 years) to access their negative cognitions, but older youngsters do report negative cognitions and thoughts about escape.

Last et al. (1992) found that in almost three-fourths of the children studied, social phobia preceded the onset of depressive disorders. D. A. Cole, Peeke, et al. (1998) astutely noted that children with social anxieties do not receive much social reinforcement. Social reinforcement tends to boost children's self-concepts and accordingly, socially anxious youngsters report lower self-concepts. D. A. Cole and his colleagues concluded that low levels of social reinforcement and lowered perceptions of self-worth are hallmark depressive characteristics. Thus, the depression may result from lowered opportunities for social reinforcement which compromise vulnerable youngsters' positive self-concepts.

## COMMON COGNITIVE CHARACTERISTICS
## AMONG ANXIOUS CHILDREN

Anxious children perceive the world in characteristic ways (Kendall et al., 1991). They vigilantly scan their internal and external worlds for signs of threat (Kendall et al., 1991; Vasey, 1993). Anxious children misinterpret relatively neutral situations and add pressure to already stressful circumstances by amplifying the threatening aspects of the environment. "Anxious children," Kendall (1992) wrote, "see the world through a template of threat and automatic questioning and they engage in dysfunctional avoidance behaviour" (p. 233). Not surprisingly, anxious youth tend to overestimate the likelihood and magnitude of anticipated dangers (Leitenberg, Yost, & Carroll-Wilson, 1986; Vasey, 1993). Moreover, anxious thinking tends to be more future-oriented and questioning in content (A. T. Beck & Clark, 1988; Lerner et al., 1999). Anxious children grossly underestimate their coping capacities (Oakley & Padesky, 1990). They engage in critical self-commentary which undermines their coping (e.g., "I can't do it"). Bell-Dolan and Wessler (1994) concluded that children's sense of their inability to cope with threat reflects an external attributional style as well as accompanying perceptions of uncontrollability.

In fact, uncontrollability is assuming primacy in developmental models of anxiety (Chorpita & Barlow, 1998). Costanzo et al. (1995) wrote, "Early experiences with an uncontrollable world are likely to be pivotal since the young child has very few a priori cognitive structures and principles that can account for changes in the environment" (pp. 86-87). Control, as defined by Chorpita and Barlow refers to the perceived capacity to influence events associated with receiving positive and negative reinforcement. Simply, a child who possesses a sense of control expects that rewards are contingent upon their actions. Costanzo et al. (1995) remarked that experiencing uncontrollable events in early childhood may render youngsters vulnerable to subsequent perceptions of uncontrollability in later childhood. Chorpita and Barlow (1998) noted that "early experiences with uncontrollable events may be thought of as a primary pathway to the development of anxiety in that such experiences may foster an increased likelihood to process events as not within one's control" (p. 5).

Not surprisingly, predictions of impending danger and catastrophic consequences are commonplace (e.g., "What if something bad happens at school"). Several authors have identified thinking errors which characterize anxious children (Epkins, 1996; Leitenberg et al., 1986). Leitenberg et al. (1986) found that anxious children had relatively high rates of overgeneralization, catastrophizing, personalization, and selective abstraction. Epkins (1996) also found that thinking errors such as personalization and overgeneralization occurred frequently in anxious youngsters. Based on the definitions of these errors found in A. T. Beck et al. (1979) , J. S. Beck (1995), and D. D. Burns (1980), various themes emerge.

Anxious youngsters tend to excessively attribute negative outcomes to themselves (personalization). Moreover, they predict the worst thing possible will happen and equate any negative outcome with disaster (catastrophizing). Further, they stretch and bend outcomes in one particular situation to erroneously fit many other dissimilar situations (overgeneralization). Finally, they selectively attend to elements reflecting unsuccessful coping or skills deficits and neglect their own potential resourcefulness in threatening situations (selective abstraction).

Many anxious youngsters think they are "on display." This heightened self-consciousness naturally truncates children's emotional flexibility and exacerbates performance pressures. These youngsters simply appear wound too tightly and believe there is a very narrow window of acceptable behavior. Accordingly, anxious children inaccurately believe they are the focus of others' attention and predict other people will notice any flaws or mistakes.

Childhood anxiety has many constituent signs and symptoms. Therapists are well-advised to address the behavioral, emotional, cognitive, physiological, and interpersonal or environmental basis of children's distress in a systematic manner. Worries and social evaluative concerns seem to be common problems. Fear of negative evaluation and perceptions of uncontrollability pervade generalized anxiety, separation anxiety, and social anxiety. Avoidance is another hallmark feature. Experiential cognitive-behavioral treatment strategies which attenuate avoidance are clearly indicated.

## INTERVENTION PLANNING

Planning treatment strategies for anxious children includes consideration of children's individual symptoms, knowledge of cognitive-behavioral strategies, and an appreciation for the *Therapeutic Exercises for Children* skills. Physiological, cognitive, emotional, behavioral, and contextual variables need to be considered in the planning process. Approaches for treating anxiety may be divided into modules. In general, therapists may wish to proceed from self-monitoring to self-instruction to exposure techniques. Exposure-based treatment is likely the most change-producing element in treating anxiety disorders (Silverman & Kurtines, 1996). Other behavioral and cognitive strategies may be regarded as facilitative strategies and lead the way toward exposure.

Treatment begins with socialization to the model. *Diamond Connections* is a gainful introduction to the cognitive model for anxious children. Anxious children tend to be expert avoiders. They may dodge their anxious feelings for a variety of reasons such as not wanting to become anxious, disappoint the therapist, or appear incompetent. Teaching anxious children that thoughts, feelings, and behaviors are the main therapeutic topics helps normalize these phenomena for youngsters. Additionally, if these feelings are normalized for youngsters, the children will be less likely to sidestep them. *Diamond Connections* gives children a road map for therapy.

Simple behavioral tasks are first steps in the therapy process. Relaxation, social skills, pleasant activity scheduling, and self-monitoring skills are common options. Completing Subjective Ratings of Distress Scales (SUDS) is a common practice in cognitive-behavioral therapy (Masters et al., 1987; Spiegler & Guevremont, 1995). *Bubble Up Your Fear* is a SUDS-like self-monitoring tool in *Therapeutic Exercises for Children*. Children list their fears in descending order and grade their level of feeling by coloring in the numbers of bubbles that correspond to the amount of fear they experience. *Bubble Up Your Fear* is a simple self-monitoring tool which may engage children in treatment. Self-monitoring techniques provide baseline information and lay the foundation for subsequent interventions. *Bubble Up Your Fear* is a relatively fun and benign way to get children talking about their fears, worries, and anxieties.

Relaxation and social skills training are good behavioral strategies for many anxious children. These options are particularly well-suited to youngsters with predominant somatic symptoms and social skills deficits (Beidel & S. M. Turner, 1998; Eisen & Silverman, 1993). *Therapeutic Exercises for Children* does not include specific exercises for relaxation and social skills training. However, many of the cognitive skills exercises may accompany relaxation and social skills training (e.g., *Bubble Up Your Fear, Catching Feelings and Thoughts, Tease Whiz, Real or False Alarms, Breaking the Crystal Ball*). Accordingly, combining some *Therapeutic Exercises for Children* techniques with these interventions may make for a comprehensive treatment package.

Cognitive self-control strategies are important facilitative skills for anxious children. *Catching Feelings and Thoughts* is a *Therapeutic Exercises for Children* drill for identifying anxiety-producing situations and recording the thoughts and feelings associated with these events. *Changing Your Tune* may be a useful vehicle for presenting self-talk to youngsters. *Breaking the Crystal Ball* focuses on modifying catastrophic thinking. The diary walks children through several questions designed to test their disastrous predictions. The completed diary provides both data to challenge the beliefs as well as a conclusion the child can use as a coping statement (e.g., "I am in charge of my fear"). By using a fortune teller metaphor, *Breaking the Crystal Ball* is an entertaining way to teach children about the fallacy of their catastrophic thinking.

Anxiety is characterized by confusion between false and real alarms (Barlow, 1993; A. T. Beck et al., 1985). In fact, for many anxious children, the "alarm is often worse than the fire" (A. T. Beck, 1976, p. 132). Consequently, it is important for children to realize the difference between real and false alarms. Accordingly, the *Real or False Alarms* diary enables children to make these distinctions. To complete the *Real or False Alarms* diary, children list the worries (alarms) they have for the week. Secondly, they keep a record of whether their worry actually came to fruition. Children then count whether their worries were real alarms or false alarms. After they complete their tally, they compare the numbers of real versus false alarms and then make a conclusion regarding this comparison. Additionally, they are taught to come up with problem-solving strategies for the real alarms.

The alert reader likely recognizes that *Breaking the Crystal Ball* and *Real or False Alarms* are not only strategies to facilitate self-control but also represent mild forms of graduated exposure. To complete each diary, the child has to confront their fears directly to some extent. Thus, the youngsters are not only developing coping statements but also simultaneously practicing facing their fears in a graduated fashion.

*Tease Whiz* is a method for helping children who are teased by their peers. *Tease Whiz* prompts children to make the distinction between other people's opinion and fact. The main focus is on empowering children so they are in charge of their own feelings. *Tease Whiz* teaches youngsters that other's opinions do not necessarily define their own identity. Imagery work serves to "shrink" the teaser. *Tease Whiz* also includes a problem-solving strategy as well as cognitive restructuring components. Of course, therapists are well-advised to integrate a social skills training component into the *Tease Whiz* skill set.

Integrating problem-solving components into the self-control exercises is important. Problem-solving strategies are implicit and explicit coping mechanisms. Secondly, it is salient for anxious children to realize that even if bad or dreaded things happen, they do have access to coping resources. Thirdly, problem-solving strategies add to the believability of coping counter-thoughts. Therapists interested in obtaining greater background in problem-solving approaches are referred to D'Zurilla (1986); Spivack, Platt, and Shure (1976); and Spivack and Shure (1982).

The worksheets and exercises are facilitative strategies designed to teach children self-control strategies. Although graduated exposure is contained in many of these exercises, children need greater opportunities for experiential learning. Therapists need to collaboratively design exposure trials where children practice their skills. More specifically, readers are referred to Silverman and Kurtines (1996), Barlow (1993), and Beidel and S. M. Turner (1998) who offer useful guidelines for drafting exposure exercises.

## IMPORTANCE OF EXPOSURE:
## COACHING CHILDREN BACK IN THE SADDLE

The importance of exposure in the treatment of anxiety disorders is well-documented (Beidel & S. M. Turner, 1998; Silverman & Kurtines, 1996; T. H. Ollendick & King, 1998). Exposure-based treatment provides children with occasions to face what they fear. Exposure is the ultimate experiential learning opportunity. While empirically well-established, the impact of exposure is also commonsensical. Indeed, when children fall off their bike, skin their knees, and subsequently avoid future bike riding, many parents knowingly encourage their children to get right back in the saddle to ride again. Accordingly, exposure-based treatment helps children get back in the saddle again.

Many cognitive-behavioral therapists believe exposure works to reduce fear through habituation (Beidel & S. M. Turner, 1998). Essentially, children learn to tolerate the discomfort associated with various stressful circumstances. As their tolerance increases, their bodily reactions such as breathing rate, flushing, and so on, decrease; and their subjective ratings of distress decline. Moreover, exposure teaches children that anxiety-producing sensations, cognitions, or stimuli have nondisastrous consequences.

Implementing an exposure-based intervention involves several considerations. Therapists should work assiduously to specifically identify the constituent elements in children's anxieties. Environmental, contextual, interpersonal, cognitive, emotional, physiological, and behavioral components should be addressed. Comprehensive exposure to cues associated with the fear is likely to lead to better outcomes (Beidel & S. M. Turner, 1998; Persons, 1989; Silverman & Kurtines, 1996).

Exposure-based treatments may be done gradually or in full intensity. Full intensity exposure is referred to as flooding (Spiegler & Guevremont, 1995). Based on our experience, we recommend graduated exposure. Before the exposure trials begin in earnest, children should have *acquired* various coping skills. The exposure trial is an opportunity for children to *apply* these acquired skills. Without the exposure trials, there is no basis for knowing whether the child can apply the skills. Moreover, as cognitive therapists, we seek to treat the children's problem in the contexts in which they occur (Spiegler & Guevremont, 1995). Exposure treatments facilitate treatment in natural settings. Through exposure, children practice transferring their skills from the therapy hour to real life contexts.

Repeated exposure trials are indicated (Beidel & S. M. Turner, 1998; Silverman & Kurtines, 1996). To illustrate this point, the first author is reminded of an old maxim from his graduate training in Behavior Therapy recommending that "Practice makes permanent." Repeated opportunities to practice the skills augment children's self-efficacy perceptions. Moreover, multiple exposure trials thicken a growing data base which challenges children's catastrophic cognitions.

Therapists are encouraged to remember the golden rule of exposure. The golden rule of exposure involves keeping the child in the anxiety-producing circumstance until a decline in responsiveness is realized (Persons, 1989). Beidel and S. M. Turner (1998) suggested that therapists adopt a 50% decline in responsiveness as a rough rule of thumb. If the exposure is terminated before the anxiety subsides, therapists risk reinforcing the child's avoidance, confirming the youngster's inaccurate beliefs, and sensitizing children to their fears.

Educating children and their parents about exposure is quite important. Collaboration with youngsters will help them increase their sense of control. We encourage therapists to let children know that they are in charge of what fears they face. Moreover, youngsters ultimately control the timing and duration of any exposure trial. We have found that using a metaphor of a captain of a team to be beneficial. As captain, the child decides the type of practice. The coach (therapist) and captain essentially develop a game plan together.

## MULTIPLE TREATMENT CONSIDERATIONS

As mentioned in Chapter 4, there can be many reasons for a child's noncompletion of homework. Many of the reasons for anxious children's noncompliance seem to be fear-based. They may fear disapproval, failure, or the thoughts and feelings associated with the task as well as the task itself. Fearing the task itself is particularly common when exposure assignments are prescribed. The behavioral avoidance shaped by the fear response is best treated by graduated tasks.

Involving a child in any exposure task is crucial. The more children perceive themselves to be in charge of the exposure the greater the likelihood for compliance. Additionally, parents can be instructed to become contingency managers (Silverman & Kurtines, 1996). Having parents participate in and contribute to their children's success decreases noncompliance. More specific methods for facilitating parent involvement are included in Chapter 8.

Overly sanitized, affectless homework completion reflects another difficulty with homework. Some anxious children may censor their responses in an effort to please therapists. In their attempts to be perfect, they may rework their worksheets so much that they dilute any therapeutic significance. In these instances, therapists are well-advised to focus on the perfectionism and fears of disapproval. If therapists ignore these issues, they run the risk of colluding with children's avoidance.

Repeated practice with the coping skills is necessary. Therapists need to teach the child there is "no magic wand" which removes their anxiety (Ginsburg, Silverman, & Kurtines, 1995). Their worries and fears do not mysteriously go away with a wave of the therapists' hand and a puff of smoke. Anxiety is diminished through diligent skills practice in anxiety-producing situations rather than through therapeutic hocus-pocus. Therefore, therapists must foster continued rehearsal so coping skills are reinforced.

No one enjoys watching an anxious child experience discomfort. Parents and therapists often have the urge to rescue the child from the anxiety-producing situation. This terminates the aversive experience for both the child and adult. While this action is temporarily satisfying, it nonetheless undermines children's self-efficacy, tolerance for discomfort, and propensity for subsequently enduring difficult tasks. Silverman and Kurtines (1996) called this penchant for rescuing youngsters "the protection trap" (p. 80).

Parents need to be educated early in treatment about exposure. They need to learn that in order for their children to improve, youngsters must face the fears they avoid and skills must be practiced in the context of negative affective arousal. Parental beliefs buttress their well-intentioned but misguided rescuing behaviors. For instance, a parent may think, "Why should my child get so upset? If I'm a good parent, I must make sure my child rarely feels bad." This natural parental inclination robs children of the opportunity to feel uncomfortable and cope with these distressing feelings. In a way, this parental propensity is a form of emotional indulgence. Consequently, children who are given this message by others learn to dread negative emotional experiences and likely avoid new, potentially anxiety-producing situations. They limit themselves to routines and familiar stimuli.

The parental beliefs which shape this overprotection can be elicited and tested by therapists. After the parents develop an alternate perspective, they are more likely to better facilitate exposure. Parents can then be more fully enlisted as contingency managers.

Therapists are also not immune to overprotection. Therapists may collude with their young clients' avoidance. For instance, they may be quite willing to simply talk about the children's worries and anxieties, and avoid concretely dealing with the issues with a *Therapeutic Exercises for Children* technique. Further, therapists may apply a *Therapeutic Exercises for Children* skill that is divorced from anxiety-producing qualities. Therapists might also avoid developing exposure tasks.

Therapists' overprotectiveness limits their effectiveness. Their beliefs mold their behavior and accordingly, therapists are encouraged to identify their beliefs associated with exposure. Often, therapists will feel guilty and erroneously think they are invalidating their clients through the exposure trials. Frequently, therapists may worry they will be overwhelmed by the child's level of anxiety and be unable to successfully manage the task. Other therapists may simply be uncomfortable with high levels of feelings in a session. More in-depth supervision and increased training in exposure-based treatment approaches can attenuate these beliefs.

## CONCLUSION

Identifying and treating anxious youngsters requires flexible application of the *Therapeutic Exercises for Children* skills. The techniques employed should be tailored to the children's idiosyncratic difficulties. Clearly, strategies addressing fears of negative evaluation and uncontrollability are productive therapeutic avenues. *Therapeutic Exercises for Children* furnishes exercises that teach children cognitive self-control skills. These techniques are facilitative tools which pave the route toward exposure. Well-integrated application of the *Therapeutic Exercises for Children* skills with behavioral exposure likely serves to decrease anxious youngsters' avoidance.

# CHAPTER 6

# Working With Depressed Children

## INTRODUCTION

Applying *Therapeutic Exercises for Children* with depressed youngsters presents several challenges to therapists. This chapter helps therapists negotiate these challenges. The chapter begins with a brief overview of the general features associated with childhood depression. An in-depth discussion of intervention planning using the *Therapeutic Exercises for Children* workbook follows. The chapter concludes with ways to manage specific clinical issues such as difficulties with agenda setting, using the skills in the context of negative affective arousal, and working with perfectionistic children.

## CLINICAL FEATURES OF DEPRESSION

While the specific manifestations of depression can vary for individual children, there are several general features which characterize most forms of the disorder. Five principal symptom clusters which explain a variety of the variance in symptoms have been identified (Ryan et al., 1987). The five factors Ryan and his colleagues identified included (a) depression/anhedonia/fatigue, (b) negative cognitions/ suicidality, (c) anxious somatic concerns, (d) appetite problems, and (e) irritability/anger. Within these clusters, the most common symptoms include depressed mood, anhedonia, problems with decision-making, anger/irritability, fatigue, insomnia, and social withdrawal. Unfounded somatic complaints such as headaches and stomachaches are quite common characteristics of depression in prepubertal children (Stark, 1990). Accompanying problems such as separation anxiety, somatic complaints, and behavior problems occur more frequently in depressed children than in depressed adolescents and adults (Birmaher et al., 1996).

The clinical characteristics of depression vary by age (Schwartz et al., 1998). For example, modal symptoms in 6- to 8-year-olds include unhappiness, decreased peer interaction and socialization, irritability, lethargy, school performance or productivity problems, accident proneness, phobias, attention seeking, and separation anxiety. Behavior problems can be a predominant feature of depression in this age group. Due to natural developmental limitations, younger children have relatively more difficulty translating their thoughts and feelings into words. Simply, they may be less able to share their depressogenic beliefs and dysphoric feelings. Consequently, they tend to communicate their depressive feelings through their behavior or conduct problems.

Schwartz et al. (1998) rightly note that with increasing psychological maturity, older elementary school children are better able to translate their thoughts and feelings into words. The average 9- to 12-year-old is more self-aware, able to share their distressing beliefs, and consequently they directly express their distressing beliefs. Thus, they may experience more typical depressive symptoms such as sad moods and self-critical thinking. However, aggression, irritability, and conduct disturbances may still characterize depression in this age. These behavior problems may be relatively more likely in children who are less accustomed to or more uncomfortable with putting their thoughts and feelings into words.

### Depressed Children's Thinking Patterns

Depressed children's thought patterns are excessively self-critical. Explanatory or attributional style is strongly correlated with depression (Gillham et al., 1995; Gladstone & Kaslow, 1995; Jaycox et al., 1994; Nolen-Hoeksema, Girgus, & Seligman, 1996; Nolen-Hoeksema et al., 1995; Seligman et al., 1995). In their groundbreaking work with adults, Abramson, Seligman, and Teasdale (1978) delineated three attributional or explanatory dimensions (internal/external, stable/unstable, global/specific). An external attribution refers to explanations that involve something about the *environment, situation, and circumstances.* An internal attribution refers to *something about the person.* Stable attributions *endure over time,* whereas unstable explanations *change or are transient over time.* Global explanations are attributions that *refer to a variety of situations* or circumstances, whereas specific attributions involve *one particular event or set of events.*

Children who explain negative events with internal, stable, and global ascriptions are more vulnerable to depression (Jaycox et al., 1994; Malcarne & Ingram, 1994; Nolen-Hoeksema & Girgus, 1995; Nolen-Hoeksema et al., 1996; Seligman et al., 1995). These children may inaccurately blame themselves for bad things happening, see causes as more permanent, and believe the stressor generalizes to all areas in their lives. These children think, "It's me, it's going to last forever, and it's going to affect everything I do" (Peterson & Seligman, 1984, p. 350).

Children who explain failure with an internal, stable, global attributional style are characterized by *pessimism* and a sense of *learned helplessness.* When faced with adversity, helplessness-oriented children give up, whereas mastery-oriented children intensify their coping efforts (Dweck, 1981). Pessimistic children respond to adversity with a distorted sense of self-blame, truncated views of change, and overgeneralizations from one event to a variety of situations. "They blame themselves for the uncontrollable," Seligman et al. (1995) remarked. "They gravitate to the most negative interpretation" (p. 169). Moreover, these youngsters blame themselves for other people's negative or hostile intentions toward them (Quiggle et al., 1992). Nolen-Hoeksema, Seligman, and Girgus (1986) examined the relationship between children's pessimistic attributional style, achievement, and depression. Children with a pessimistic explanatory style were more depressed and helpless in the classroom. Further, they scored lower on achievement measures. These children took excessive personal responsibility for failure and distanced themselves from success.

Nolen-Hoeksema and Girgus (1995) concluded that children's pessimistic attributional style is established by 9 years old. However, while the negative explanatory set may be in place by 9 years of age, its pernicious effect may not be pronounced until a few years later. J. E. Turner and D. A. Cole (1994) found that the negative effect associated with the attributional style was more striking in 8th graders than in either 4th or 6th graders. Thus, attributional style may exert a stronger mediating influence on older children's behavior and emotions.

### Depressed Children's Social and Interpersonal Difficulties

Depressed children's hallmark passivity and withdrawal are likely associated with perceptions of uncontrollability (Quiggle et al., 1992).

Quiggle and her colleagues remarked that depressed children see their passivity and withdrawal as viable options leading to positive outcomes. Simply, passivity and withdrawal are negatively reinforcing for them. When they withdraw from others, they perceive themselves as able to escape and subsequently exact control over anticipated criticism and rejection. Consequently, the passivity and withdrawal serves a protective function for them.

Depressed children experience considerably more social difficulties than their nondepressed peers. Nolen-Hoeksema and Girgus (1995) reported that repeated failures in school and with peers buttress a pessimistic and helpless explanatory style. Kolko (1987) reported that depressed children are described by others as more unpopular, socially withdrawn, unathletic, and unattractive. Moreover, they are seen as less outgoing and helpful. Kovacs and Goldston (1991) noted that depressed children's withdrawal promotes problems initiating and reciprocating social exchanges. Rudolph, Hammen, and Burge (1997) found that depressed children had more pessimistic predictions regarding interpersonal outcomes as well as perceived themselves to be less competent and deserving in relationships. Not surprisingly, depressed children's irritability and problems with eye contact dissuades friend-making overtures by peers (Kovacs & Goldston, 1991). "Social environments likely to be depressogenic," Weisz et al. (1992) concluded, "are those in which children repeatedly receive feedback that makes them doubt their own competence or in which the outcomes children experience at the hands of adults and others appear to occur non-contingently capriciously or both" (p. 417).

Quiggle et al. (1992) noted that both aggressive and depressive children tended to have a cognitive bias which emphasized undue attention to the negative cues in their environment. Aggressive children typically interpret social situations in a hostile manner and blame other people (Dodge, 1985). On the other hand, depressed youngsters tend to blame themselves. Quiggle and her colleagues wrote that aggressive children expect that aggression will effectively resolve the problem whereas depressed children believe nothing they can do will resolve the situation. Further, Quiggle continued that aggressive children value aggression as an easy yet effective response to conflict. Therefore, based on their own notions about aggressive behavior, aggressive children react to interpersonal conflict with hostile, attacking behavior whereas depressed children respond with passivity and withdrawal.

Depressive symptoms combine into a complex and often debilitating symptom network. Cognitive, behavioral, emotional, physiological, and interpersonal problems commingle, complicating treatment. Moreover, symptom pictures vary per age. Thus, intervention planning with the *Therapeutic Exercises for Children* material must account for a variety of symptoms and presenting complaints.

## INTERVENTION PLANNING

Systematic treatment planning gives therapy a necessary intentional focus. Good planning allows therapists to properly time interventions, predict obstacles, develop contingency plans, and be efficient with time and resources. Breaking therapy into constituent sections or modules may be a helpful template (Freeman, 1998). Case conceptualization will facilitate intervention planning and individualized treatment. The planning process should consider physiological, cognitive, emotional, behavioral, and conceptual variables.

In general, treatment for depressed youngsters begins with socialization to the model and simple cognitive-behavioral techniques such as pleasant activity scheduling, problem-solving, and social skills training. Identification of feelings and accompanying thoughts represent the next module. Learning to evaluate inaccurate thoughts and construct more adaptive counter-thoughts is a third module. Designing behavioral experiments where children test and enact their new assumptions is a fourth module. Many *Therapeutic Exercises for Children* skills may be helpful in each of these modules.

Pessimism, hopelessness, and suicidality are clear first-treatment targets. However, the *Therapeutic Exercises for Children* skills are not primary intervention tools for suicidal children. In these cases, therapists must complete a risk assessment and follow customary standards of care. For nonsuicidal but pessimistic children who believe nothing they can do will help them and nothing will change their dismal situation, therapists must strive to instill hope. Socialization exercises like *Diamond Connections* and priming exercises like *Permanent or Temporary* and *Sticks and Stones* may be in order in the early stages of treatment for these youngsters. These activities are relatively simple, nonthreatening, and fun. They can be used not only for priming but also as a way to increase children's pleasant activity.

*PANDY Fun Diary* is a way for children and their families to schedule pleasant activities. Parental reinforcement adds to this activity for depressed youngsters. Children get to do something that, prior to being depressed, was fun, and earn reinforcement from their parents for following through with this activity.

Mouse traps and fix-it sheets are problem-solving strategies included in *Therapeutic Exercises for Children*. The skills help youngsters categorize problems into behavioral, cognitive, and affective terms. Additionally, the exercises walk the youngsters through various problem-solving steps. Social skills are not specifically taught via *Therapeutic Exercises for Children*. However, social skills training approaches (Conger & Keane, 1981; Polyson & Kimball, 1993) can be readily integrated into the exercises.

Reliably identifying feelings paves the route for subsequent cognitive intervention. The *Diamond Connections* worksheet is a handy method for identifying feelings. Additionally, the *PANDY Coloring Sheets* also teach children to record feelings. Further, therapists can assign the situation, feeling, and feeling signal columns on the *Catching Feelings and Thoughts* diary as another way to educate children about feelings.

Cognitive priming activities shift children's perceptual set. The priming activities do not directly address cognitive content but rather focus on modifying cognitive process (Riskind, 1991; Riskind, Sarampote, & Mercier, 1996). Priming activities may be used as either precursors to thought testing or in conjunction with thought testing techniques with depressed children. *Permanent or Temporary, Sticks and Stones,* and *Many Meanings* are examples of priming techniques in *Therapeutic Exercises for Children*. The priming techniques loosen children's rigid thinking processes by expanding children's perspectives.

Identifying negative automatic thoughts and connecting them to distressing feelings is a necessary precursor to thought testing. *Catching Feelings and Thoughts* diaries are thought records for children. Helping children identify emotionally meaningful thoughts is crucial in this module. If youngsters are unable to identify the distressing cognitions, the thought testing techniques will fall flat. Also, if children identify thoughts — but these beliefs are not related to distressing emotions — therapists run the risk of doing great work with meaningless thoughts (Padesky, 1988). Thus, therapists must help youngsters dig for the specific thoughts that are associated with their depressed feelings.

Clinical experience suggests depressed children have difficulty identifying automatic thoughts. Therapists should gently nudge this process along and resist the urge to begin thought testing until they are confident a meaningful thought is identified. Often, digging under the surface of the initially reported thoughts in order to obtain psychologically salient material is necessary. The following transcript illustrates the process.

*Jamie:* I really hate it when my friends get together.
*Therapist:* I'm not sure what you mean.
*Jamie:* They really bug me.
*Therapist:* In what ways do they bug you?
*Jamie:* Just the things they do. They talk to each other. Kind of whisper. They have a lot of "in" jokes.
*Therapist:* How do you feel when they do the things that bug you?
*Jamie:* Depressed.
*Therapist:* So when you feel depressed, what goes through your mind?
*Jamie:* They are jerks to be acting like this.
*Therapist:* When they tell jokes and whisper to each other, what does that mean about you?
*Jamie:* They're shutting me out. I don't fit in. (Tears well up in eyes)
*Therapist:* Let's say this were true. What would it mean if they truly saw you as an outsider?
*Jamie:* I don't know. Maybe I can't measure up to them.
*Therapist:* So when you think you can't measure up, how do you feel?
*Jamie:* Really bummed.
*Therapist:* Let me see if I understand. You see your friends making lots of "in" jokes and whispering. You feel really depressed and you say to yourself "I am an outsider and I can't measure up to them."

This transcript has several salient points. First, the therapist demonstrates considerable patience and models appropriate therapeutic pacing. Secondly, the therapist queried the child for specific information and linked thoughts with feelings. Thirdly, the therapist probed until an emotional reaction was elicited. Fourth, once the depressogenic thought was identified, the therapist went back to the child and checked out whether this thought was indeed strongly associated with his depressed feeling.

Once depressed children can identify their thoughts, therapists may proceed to the thought testing module. Thought testing procedures, exercises, and activities should be applied gradually beginning with simple, inelegant procedures and progressing with more complex, elegant interventions. Moreover, the thought testing should be tailored to specific children and types of beliefs. For example, simple, inelegant techniques are best-suited to younger, more distressed children who benefit from more concrete interventions (Ronen, 1998).

The *Changing Your Tune* skill set is a self-instructional approach. Self-instructional approaches focus on modifying internal dialogue by replacing maladaptive cognitions with more adaptive ones (Meichenbaum, 1985). Accordingly, the *Changing Your Tune* skills do not require in-depth rational analysis. Children are simply instructed to create more productive things they can say to themselves. These self-instructional type approaches seem best-suited to the early phases of treatment. Moreover, these techniques provide the groundwork for more complex tasks.

Tests of evidence are classic cognitive therapy interventions. Tests of evidence are relatively complex tasks and require depthful rational analysis. Not surprisingly, tests of evidence are effortful techniques tapping considerable mental energy. The tasks demands may be too overwhelming for a depressed child early in treatment. A severely depressed child is unlikely to access the psychological resources a test of evidence demands. Tests of evidence call for focused attention, verbal fluency, and frustration tolerance. Accordingly, tests of evidence are considered complex and elegant tasks for children.

*Clue Snooping* is the *Therapeutic Exercises for Children* skill that most resembles a test of evidence. Clue snooping entails examining the facts that support a belief and the facts that do not support a belief. After their review of the evidence, children then reach a conclusion. Children can write their conclusion on coping cards and review them on an as-needed basis. The depth of processing required in a test of evidence can facilitate enduring change. By completing a test of evidence, children learn how to evaluate their thoughts as well as construct an alternative response. The level of analysis in a test of evidence promotes change in cognitive processes and cognitive content.

*Thought Digger* is another advanced technique used to facilitate the self-questioning and self-evaluative process. *Thought Digger* helps depressed youngsters craft better questions to challenge their negative automatic thoughts. In essence, *Thought Digger* emphasizes children's internalization of the Socratic Dialogue or questions therapists may ask them when evaluating thoughts. Cognitive process as well as cognitive content are therapeutic foci. Children learn questions to ask themselves as well as constructing new responses. The basic act of questioning thoughts compels children to stop and think things over. By stopping to question their appraisals, the automatic nature of negative thoughts can be interrupted.

The self-questioning process is a difficult one for children to acquire. First, negative thoughts are usually well-practiced, habitual, stream of conscious cognitive products. Accordingly, due to the automatic nature of these beliefs, children do not evaluate them, they simply accept their veracity. Thus, exposing youngsters to the importance of doubting their negative internal dialogue is clinically salient. Second, children often do not have access to many questions that could challenge their automatic thoughts. By providing questions for them, *Thought Digger* expands their supply of questions. Third, children need to know when to ask themselves questions. *Thought Digger* provides youngsters with information regarding the when, what, and how of self-questioning.

Behavioral experiments reinforce changes achieved through the skills. Behavioral experiments are forms of exposure and serve as disconfirming evidence. For example, a depressed girl expects that everyone will reject her. The cognitive work may help her construct an alternative view such as "Some kids will reject me but most children will not." Since the new belief has less experience and data supporting it than the old belief does, the child needs to collect data confirming the new perspective. Thus, the child can be encouraged to say "Hi" to 10 people and record their reactions. After the experiment is completed, the child then compares the data to her belief (e.g., "How many people said 'Hi' back or smiled?" "How many did nothing?" "How many people said something bad back to her or teased her?" "Was her prediction that most people would reject her true?").

Depressed children's counter-thoughts should also include a problem-solving component. The behavioral experiments can foster problem-solving strategies. For instance, in the previous example, the depressed girl needed to have a plan to cope with any rejection she experienced. Accordingly, if 1 child out of 10 teased her and was "mean" towards her, the girl needed a way to handle the teasing (e.g., "Some kids will tease me, but I could ignore them"). Ignoring can be practiced in session. Graduated homework may include instructing the girl to banter with her stuffed animals as a first step. Next, the girl could practice assertiveness skills. Finally, graduated experiments where the youngster can try out her problem-solving strategies are assigned. The behavioral experiments and problem-solving strategies greatly increase the counter-thoughts' believability.

## ADDITIONAL CLINICAL CONSIDERATIONS

### Difficulty Setting Agendas

Children who are depressed, pessimistic, or hopeless may have considerable difficulty setting agendas. Their passivity and withdrawal may contribute to a lack of investment in treatment. Often, when asked what they want to work on, these youngsters might shrug and say, "I don't know, you decide." More specifically, more directiveness early in treatment with these youngsters is indicated. Rather than giving an open-ended choice to the depressed youngster (e.g., "What would you like to work on?"), the therapist may elect to give a forced choice (e.g., "Would you prefer to work on the problems you are having with your friends or your difficulty with homework?"). Open-ended formats which include wearisome possibilities may overwhelm a very depressed youngster. They simply may not have the energy or confidence to choose between many options. Thus, the forced choice format is a simpler task for depressed children. Therapists may also encourage reluctant children to find ways to take charge. Agenda setting can be explained as a way to take charge of therapy. Additionally, therapists may elect to review the advantages and disadvantages of agenda setting with hesitant children. Examining the pros and cons of agenda setting with children disinclined toward agenda setting may be quite empowering. Having an adult listen to their objections may dilute their unwillingness to establish agendas.

### Using Skills in the Context of
### Negative Emotional Arousal

Cognitive therapists believe change that occurs in the context of negative affective arousal is most enduring (Persons, 1989; Robins & Hayes, 1993). Children who experiment with these newly acquired coping skills when they are truly distressed are more likely to experience enduring change. Accordingly, therapists need to help depressed youngsters apply their coping skills when they are depressed.

Children may frequently say they were too depressed to do a thought record or some other cognitive-behavioral skill. Alert therapists avoid colluding with this belief. In fact, the belief "I am too depressed to do any of these skills" is grist for the therapeutic mill. Therapists and children could work together to set this belief up as an experiment. The task could be broken down into graduated parts and the child could try to do at least one part. If the child accomplished any part of the task, the activity casts doubt on the belief.

Therapists must not be content with teaching the skills to children when they are not distressed. The acquisition of skills can occur in an emotionally neutral state, however, application necessitates affective arousal. Many depressed youngsters usually show up in the therapist's office feeling badly. In these cases, applying the coping skills to dysphoric moods is relatively straightforward.

Some children may present without any noticeable negative affect. They may be inhibiting their negative feelings or simply be out of touch with their internal states. In these instances, therapists are well-advised to teach youngsters pathways to identify, tolerate, and accept their feelings. Frequently, accurate empathy often amplifies these feelings and facilitates emotional expression. Once these feelings pop out, the skills can then be applied to the distressing feelings.

Cognitive therapy is a very experiential treatment approach (Knell, 1993). Skills are practiced with a here-and-now perspective. A here-and-now focus facilitates skills practice with immediate emotional experiences. Practicing cognitive therapy coping skills in the therapeutic moment when children cry, become frustrated, or get anxious adds to therapeutic potential. When negative feelings arise in session, the coping skills can be applied to the distress. The naturally occurring negative feelings are graduated exposure trials. Children master their distress in small bits through the cognitive skills practice.

## Working With Perfectionistic Children

Perfectionism can exacerbate self-critical cognitions, perceptions of self-doubt, and strong anxious and depressed feelings. Perfectionism paralyzes youngsters causing them to equate mistakes with failure (Kendall et al., 1992). The perfectionism inhibits behavior and truncates goal attainment. Bandura (1977b) claimed that individuals who overaspire and underachieve are particularly prone to maladjustment. Their goals are set too high, they inevitably fail to achieve attainable goals, and consequently, their perceptions of personal competence are lowered (Bandura, 1977b; Rotter, 1982).

Setting appropriate goals for perfectionistic children is vitally important. These children's goals are terribly "out of whack" and need proper adjustment. Establishing goals which facilitate success and mastery is a primary task. Small steps along the way to large accomplishments need to be outlined. Therapists need to eschew goals that imply emotional perfectionism (e.g., never feeling sad, eliminating nervousness).

Attending to perfectionistic beliefs is another central therapeutic task. The *Catching Feelings and Thoughts* diary is a good method for identifying the beliefs that buttress perfectionistic behavior. For example, "Even one mistake means I'm stupid" may be reported by youngsters. Once these beliefs are identified, therapists can apply several *Therapeutic Exercises for Children* cognitive skills to the inaccurate thinking. *Changing Your Tune, Thought Digger, Clue Snooping,* and *Breaking the Crystal Ball* are examples of techniques that can be applied to these problems.

Finally, gradual exposure to imperfectionism is indicated. Exposure to imperfect models is a good first step. Recognizing other people's mistakes normalizes errors. Children could be given the assignment to observe and record other people making a mistake. They could watch parents, teachers, friends, or television characters do something wrong, and then record their own thoughts and feelings which accompany these miscues.

Moreover, spotting other people's mistakes is a form of graduated exposure. For some children who are sensitive to mistakes, simply considering errors may be anxiety producing or depressing. Thus, therapists should process even these seemingly minor assignments. Therapeutic processing questions could include:

- What is it like for you to see _____ making a mistake?
- What went through your mind when _____ made a mistake?
- How did it make you feel?
- What happened after they made a mistake?

After the child has learned some coping skills, more direct exposure is indicated. Children should be encouraged to make mistakes in their mousework. Words could be misspelled or their handwriting could be sloppy. They could be encouraged to make small mistakes that people may notice. For example, they might wear a wrist watch upside down or put a black pen cap on a blue pen. These initial experiences would then be followed by more noticeable mistakes such as wearing different colored socks, eating with the opposite hand, and other behavioral experiments.

## CONCLUSION

Childhood depression presents in multifaceted ways. Since it is not a monolithic disorder, a one-size-fits-all strategy is impractical. Thus, implementing workbook techniques in a polished manner requires considerable thoughtfulness. Care should be exercised in sequencing *Therapeutic Exercises for Children* interventions which ameliorate cognitive, emotional, behavioral, physiological, and interpersonal symptoms.

*Therapeutic Exercises for Children* offers therapists a wide array of skill sets. Selecting the proper skill set which matches the child's problem area is a central task for therapists. The intervention sequencing section gives therapists broad guidelines for the timing of each skill set. Finally, encouraging depressed youngsters to use the skills when they are feeling badly is crucial. Applying the skills in context of negative arousal communicates that the skills are important, represent real-world practice, and subsequently build genuine self-efficacy.

# CHAPTER 7

# Using *Therapeutic Exercises for Children* With Groups

## INTRODUCTION

Group therapy may represent an efficient and effective medium to apply the *Therapeutic Exercises for Children* skills. There is growing interest in delivering cognitive-behavioral therapy to groups of children (Albano & Barlow, 1996; Albano & DiBartolo, 1997; R. D. Friedberg et al., 1999; Ginsburg et al., 1995; Kendall et al., 1992; Kendall, MacDonald, & Treadwell, 1995; Silverman & Kurtines, 1996). This chapter alerts therapists to the advantages, issues, and considerations which accompany group work with *Therapeutic Exercises for Children*. Session structure, setting limits, and balancing psychoeducation and psychotherapy are addressed. Finally, specific examples of using *Therapeutic Exercises for Children* with groups of children are provided.

## ADVANTAGES OF USING
## *THERAPEUTIC EXERCISES FOR CHILDREN*
## WITH GROUPS

Group treatment for depressed and anxious children offers several advantages to clinicians. Many of the *Therapeutic Exercises for Children* skills were initially developed for delivery in a group format. Group therapy provides an opportunity for therapists to reach a large number of children. Further, hearing other children express their sad and worried feelings normalizes emotional expression for youngsters.

Other children are readily available peer models in group therapy. Finally, depressed and anxious youngsters are commonly lonely, withdrawn, and hypersensitive to criticism and rejection. Group therapy provides a medium in which these thoughts and feelings can readily be identified and modified. However, despite the advantages of group therapy, clinicians must consider whether a group format is the right option for each individual child. This chapter addresses several salient issues confronting therapists who use *Therapeutic Exercises for Children* with groups of children.

## CAUTIONS FOR GROUP THERAPY

There are only a few cautions to using *Therapeutic Exercises for Children* in groups. First, the children in the group must have sufficient self-control to profit from group interaction. Thus, if the child has difficulty paying attention, staying in their seat, or keeping their hands and feet to themselves, therapists may want to postpone this option until greater self-regulation is achieved. Additionally, children who are acutely and severely distressed may need more individual attention. A child burdened by vegetative depressive symptoms and weighed down by severe hopelessness requires individual therapy and possibly medication. Group therapy might be considered as a subsequent option. Similarly, children whose anxiety is so severe as to create torturous shyness, fatiguing vigilance, and debilitating self-doubts may need individual treatment prior to beginning group work.

## GROUP COMPOSITION

Multiple factors may influence group composition. Ideally, the group reflects a healthy mixture of gender and ethnicity. However, depending on referral patterns, a robust mix may not be realistic. Regardless of the actual numbers, therapists must ensure a psychologically safe and emotionally facilitative milieu where gender and ethnic differences are respected. Age, grade level, and psychological maturity are other important group composition variables. Age and grade level seem less salient than maturity level. For instance, a mature 3rd grader may profit by being the youngest child in the group. The older children who have similar problems may serve as coping models for the youngster. On the other hand, being the oldest in a group predominately composed of younger children may contribute to a child's reluctance or lack of investment in the group. An older child who looks around and sees only younger children may think he or she is too old for the group. These beliefs likely represent ripe therapeutic material and are appropriate therapeutic foci. The older child might be empowered by taking a leadership role within the group.

In real-life practice settings, heterogeneous groups are more the rule than the exception. Therapists will likely need to juggle the complex needs of different children who attend their group. While equal distribution of children in the group is ideal, varying composition patterns are likely. Thus, considerable therapeutic skill is necessary for effective group intervention.

## OPEN VERSUS CLOSED ENROLLMENT

Therapists need to decide whether their groups will have a closed enrollment or an open enrollment format. In closed enrollment, the group composition stays the same throughout the course of the group. No new members are added after the first week or so once the group begins. In open enrollment, children are admitted to the group at any point in time. Thus, the group composition continually changes over the course of the group.

In our PANDY Program, we elected to have closed group enrollment for several reasons. In each group, skills are presented in a graduated manner with each skill building on the previous one. If the children have not all been exposed to the same training in group, skill acquisition and application becomes trickier. Secondly, with constantly changing group composition, group cohesion may be more difficult to attain. If new children are constantly being folded into the group, there will be a greater variability in functioning level. Children who enter after a group has begun may become overwhelmed. Therapists are wise to consider these and other relevant possibilities before they decide on an open or closed format.

## SESSION STRUCTURE

The basic session structure described in the individual therapy chapter also holds true for group counseling. Agenda setting helps structure the group format, allowing content and process to emerge. Agendas are collaboratively established and implemented. Eliciting feedback from the children at the end of each group continues to be an important therapeutic task in group therapy. In this way, children can observe their peers giving positive and negative feedback to adults with relative impunity. Certainly, mousework assignments are as central in group work as they are in individual work. Homework provides the between-session practice that augments the within-session work.

## SETTING LIMITS AND DEFINING RULES

Children need limits from their therapists. Letting children know the rules of therapy creates comfort and security. Enforcing these limits forges consistency and reinforces trust. Children learn what to expect from the therapist.

Rules and limits in therapy allow the therapeutic process to unfold. Accordingly, in our PANDY groups, defining group rules is a first major task. We generally begin with several prepared rules (e.g., keeping hands and feet to oneself, listening when others talk). Although these rules were created by the therapists, we try to encourage the children to collaborate. For example, children are asked if they know what each rule means and if they agree with it. Going over the rules does not have to be a dry exercise. Rather, we invite them to cheer each rule they agree with and boo any rule they disagree with. After the prepared group rules are discussed, the children are given opportunities to include their own rules. We believe this fosters greater investment in the group and empowers the children. Moreover, giving children the chance to construct their own rules enables genuine collaboration.

Once the salient rules are established, therapists must enforce the limits. If therapists do not enforce the limits, the group process will likely be compromised. Additionally, if limits are established and therapists are reluctant to apply them, children may lose faith in the therapists. Therapists who do not do what they promise lose credibility. Once this credibility and concomitant trust erodes, treatment becomes more difficult.

Limit-setting should be processed with group members. If limits are set with one child in group, therapists may elect to process the limit-setting with other group members as well (e.g., "What was it like for you to see me tell Jimmy to sit back down in his seat?"). This may be an especially useful strategy for children who fear being reprimanded or making a mistake. Accordingly, there is plentiful opportunity for vicarious learning. Youngsters can see that even though a child was reprimanded, the therapists did not negatively evaluate him or her.

## PSYCHOEDUCATION AND PSYCHOTHERAPY

Our PANDY groups strike a balance between psychotherapy and psychoeducation. The psychoeducation component involves skill *acquisition*. Group leaders teach skills that children can *apply* to their problems. Direct teaching of coping skills is a necessary precursor to skill application. Applying acquired skills in the context of negative arousal is a vital focus for psychotherapy.

The PANDY group balances psychoeducational instruction with psychotherapeutic application. Children are taught skills such as self-monitoring, pleasant activity scheduling, various cognitive techniques, priming methods, and behavioral skills. Through the group process, children are encouraged to use these skills when problematic feelings arise. Moreover, a group format provides a naturalistic context for rehearsing acquired skills.

Group therapists are advised to focus on teaching coping skills and then use the group milieu to practice these tools. If the coping skills are taught simply on an abstract, intellectual basis, treatment may be less likely to generalize. Additionally, if the children have opportunities to acquire skills in group, therapists are likely to see the difficulties children experience in applying them. If therapists witness skill application difficulties, they have the opportunity to preempt these problems. Moreover, opportunities for real-life application builds genuine self-confidence. In this way, the skills become more portable for the youngsters. They carry the techniques with them from situation to situation.

## USING GROUP PROCESS WITH
### *THERAPEUTIC EXERCISES FOR CHILDREN*

Group therapy offers an often lively here-and-now milieu in which to acquire and apply the *Therapeutic Exercises for Children* skills. Depressed and anxious youngsters commonly hold beliefs that are embedded in interpersonal processes. Thoughts such as "I'm a dork, I don't fit in, Nobody likes me, Other kids will make fun of me, I'm a psycho maniac," are inherently tied to interpersonal behavior. The group enables therapists to directly test these maladaptive assumptions.

Alert cognitive therapists will use the group process as a social learning laboratory. The way children interact with peers and interpret these interactions are fruitful therapeutic foci. Group therapy is a natural exposure trial for these children. Skillful therapists will pinpoint salient moments in the group interaction and use these samples of behavior to teach or reinforce *Therapeutic Exercises for Children* skills. Many anxious and depressed children fear negative evaluation. They expect to be ignored, rejected, discounted, or humiliated. Their fear is often so intense that they avoid social situations. Thus, their expectations gain strength because they are rarely tested and disconfirmed.

The simple act of completing a worksheet can represent a graduated exposure trial for a child who fears negative evaluation by others. The child can be invited to read their worksheet aloud and share their responses with peers. The child's thoughts and feelings about reading aloud can be elicited. The following transcript material illustrates the process.

| | |
|---|---|
| *Therapist:* | So Jenny, what was it like to share your worksheet? |
| *Jenny:* | Sort of scary. |
| *Therapist:* | What zipped into your mind? |
| *Jenny:* | Everybody will think I'm a dork. |
| *Therapist:* | That's a scary thought. It kind of sounds like the things that go through your mind at school. |
| *Jenny:* | Yeah, it's just like that. |
| *Therapist:* | Would you be willing to check and see whether your guess about what everybody thinks about you is true? |
| *Jenny:* | I'm not sure. |
| *Therapist:* | I know it's a little scary. Would it be easier if the other group members help you? |
| *Jenny:* | Maybe. |
| *Therapist:* | Okay. Let's check it out. Is everybody willing to help Jenny? |

Jenny's fears of negative evaluation are emitted in an emotional, here-and-now context. The therapist can help Jenny test out her predictions regarding others' reactions to her. Therapists can then encourage Jenny to ask the group for feedback. If this is too difficult, the therapist can ask the group for her. After the data are gathered, Jenny can be asked to make sense of the experience. The transcript presented below illustrates the process.

*Therapist:* Jenny, do you want to ask if the other group members think you are a dork?

*Jenny:* I'm not sure.

*Therapist:* It is a little frightening to do. Do you want me to help you?

*Jenny:* Yes.

*Therapist:* Jenny is worried that you think she is a dork. Jenny, do you have a guess or estimate about how many group members think you are a dork?

*Jenny:* Everybody.

*Therapist:* Jenny guesses that all of you think she is a dork. Let's check it out. Raise your hand if you think she is a dork. (No one raises their hand)

*Therapist:* Jenny, how many children raised their hand?

*Jenny:* (Smiling) None.

*Therapist:* What does that mean about your guess?

Many therapists may be reluctant to try this experiment in groups because they fear eliciting negative feedback. However, if some children did raise their hand in agreement with Jenny's negative prediction, the experiment can still be quite successful. In fact, it could be argued that the experience may be potentiated by the negative feedback. Some negative feedback makes the experience more realistic.

If some children raise their hand and say they think Jenny is a dork, the therapist should ask them for clarification (e.g., "What is a dork?" "How does Jenny act like that?"). After the feedback is clarified, the therapist then encourages Jenny to review and consider the feedback. It is important to teach children to critically evaluate others' feedback rather than blindly accepting it. The therapist can then help Jenny by asking, "What parts do you disagree with?" The *Tease Whiz* skills are also helpful in processing the negative feedback. These skills can help children make the important distinctions between other people's opinion and fact. The group experience may further help the youngsters distinguish between fact and opinion. The therapists might ask the child, "Who made Billy the expert on being a dork?" "How do you know that Ramon knows what a dork is?" "How did Brandy become in charge of defining who you are?"

In our experience, anxious and depressed children tend to give each other positive or at least neutral feedback. While this is comfortable, it may not be the most change producing. Children who fear negative evaluation likely have directly experienced criticism and disapproval. Since the beliefs are buttressed by learning histories, a direct, new, disconfirming experience is necessary. Therefore, we recommend that if no negative feedback is given, therapists raise the issue themselves, and invite the youngsters to consider this possibility. The following transcript illustrates the process.

| | |
|---|---|
| *Therapist:* | So nobody thinks Jenny is a dork. But let me ask you something, Jenny. What if somebody had said you were a dork? |
| *Jenny:* | That would be terrible. |
| *Therapist:* | What would be terrible about that? |
| *Jenny:* | I'd feel bad. |
| *Therapist:* | What would go through your mind? |
| *Jenny:* | Kids think I'm a dork. |
| *Therapist:* | Now, remember I asked what if one kid agreed you were a dork. Would it make a difference if one kid thought you were a dork and four kids didn't? |
| *Jenny:* | I don't think so. I'm not sure. |
| *Therapist:* | Well, let's see if we can figure this out. Did more kids say you were a dork or did more kids say you weren't a dork? |
| *Jenny:* | More kids said I wasn't. |
| *Therapist:* | What does that say to you? |
| *Jenny:* | Most kids don't think I'm a dork. But one kid does! |
| *Therapist:* | And you are paying attention to that one kid, and forgetting about the others. |
| *Jenny:* | I guess so. |
| *Therapist:* | If you were really a dork, would most kids think so or just one? |
| *Jenny:* | Most kids. |
| *Therapist:* | What does this mean? |
| *Jenny:* | Since most kids don't think I'm a dork, I'm probably not one. But what about the kid who thought I was a dork? |
| *Therapist:* | What question could you ask yourself about that? |
| *Jenny:* | Who made him the expert? (Laughs) |

## CAUTIONS IN THERAPEUTIC PROCESSING

Therapeutic processing in groups can be very impactful. However, therapists are well-advised to consider several cautions. First, therapists must ascertain whether the group members are able to tolerate the anxiety associated with group interaction and feedback. For shy, withdrawn, and avoidant children, giving and receiving feedback can be initially torturous. Therapists then need to graduate the demands for feedback. Secondly, therapists need to determine children's skill levels. Children with poorer social skills and limited expressive skills will have initial difficulty giving and receiving feedback. Thirdly, therapists must work assiduously to help the children successfully interpret the feedback. Accordingly, therapists are encouraged to take an active stance in directing the feedback.

## CONCLUSION

Applying *Therapeutic Exercises for Children* in a group format offers several therapeutic opportunities to children. As Kendall et al. (1995) noted, "Youth are known for their responsiveness to and concern about peers" (p. 579). A group format allows for skill rehearsal in a relatively naturalistic setting. Children practice social skills with other children. Secondly, the group format provides a ripe chance to test out their concerns regarding social evaluation. Finally, being in a group normalizes the counseling experience for many children. Thus, the group format adds another dimension to work with *Therapeutic Exercises for Children*.

**CHAPTER 8**

# Working With Parents

## INTRODUCTION

Working with parents is a key ingredient in enhancing *Therapeutic Exercises for Children*. Keeping parents and their children literally and figuratively on the same page allows therapists greater flexibility with the workbook. This chapter briefly presents some salient parental variables associated with childhood depression and anxiety. Further, recommendations for working with parents whose children use *Therapeutic Exercises for Children* are made. Finally, the chapter includes parent training resources for clinicians and ways of providing feedback to parents.

## PARENTAL VARIABLES IN CHILDHOOD ANXIETY AND DEPRESSION

Family stress and conflict place children at risk for depression (P. M. Cole & Kaslow, 1988; Kaslow & Rascusin, 1990). In fact, the degree of psychosocial adversity predicted the level of impairment in children with Generalized Anxiety Disorder (GAD) (Manassis & Hood, 1998). Parental maltreatment of their children damages children's nascent self-esteem and identity development (Schaefer & Millman, 1981). Stark, Rouse, and Livingstone (1991) concluded that depression in young children is associated with ruptures in family environments such as parental drug abuse and domestic violence. Intense marital conflict punctuated by bitter exchanges and openly hostile behavior between partners contribute to children's depression.

Children of depressed parents have a greater likelihood of becoming depressed (Beardslee & Wheelock, 1994; Beardslee et al., 1993). Children whose parents are depressed are approximately three times more likely to develop depression than children who do not have a depressive disorder (Birmaher et al., 1996). The percent of children who eventually became depressed themselves ranges from 11% to 50% (Beardslee et al., 1997). Thus, parents' depression must be addressed in treatment.

Nolen-Hoeksema et al. (1995) suggested that the quality of interaction between vulnerable children and their depressed parents may be more important than diagnostic status. Parents of depressed children tend to be rejecting or overly intrusive in their children's lives (P. M. Cole & Kaslow, 1988). Depressed mothers demonstrate more negative affect interacting with their babies than nondepressed mothers (Beardslee & Wheelock, 1994). Nolen-Hoeksema et al. (1995) found that mothers with high levels of negative affect tended to have children who had lower levels of frustration tolerance and persistence. Simply, children may quit the task to avoid parents' ridicule and the quitting prompts increased parental ridicule (Nolen-Hoeksema et al., 1995). Overly intrusive parenting styles may also promote children's learned helplessness. Nolen-Hoeksema et al. (1995) noted, "If parents respond to their children's difficulties by intruding and solving their children's problems for them, parents may limit their children's opportunities to learn persistence and new ways of approaching problems" (p. 378).

Familial psychiatric history is a factor that may increase children's vulnerability to anxiety. Children whose mothers suffered from Overanxious Disorder (OAD) in childhood had a greater risk for anxiety disorders (Bernstein & Borchardt, 1991). Bell-Dolan et al. (1990) found that substance abuse in fathers increased the risk for anxiety disorders in children. Bell-Dolan and her colleagues concluded that the alcohol abuse may be an environmental stressor for children which increases their anxiety due to the father's unpredictable and often aggressive behavior. Moreover, they added the father's alcohol may also be a form of self-medication for an anxiety disorder.

In a study with elementary school children ages 7 to 12 years old, Beidel and S. M. Turner (1997) found that children whose parents had an anxiety disorder were 5.4 times more vulnerable to developing an anxiety disorder than their counterparts. Beidel and S. M. Turner also aptly concluded that the relationship between parental psychopathology and childhood anxiety may be affected by socioeconomic level. The link between parental psychopathology and childhood anxiety disorders was strongest among low socioeconomic status (SES) families. Beidel and S. M. Turner argued that low SES is a factor that clearly increases stress levels, and would increase family members' anxiety.

Lee and Gotlib (1989) commented that depressed parents' acute state of self-focused attention blinds them to their children's emotional needs. "Parenting is significantly impaired," Beardslee and Wheelock (1994) wrote, "through the mechanism of decreased attention and less intensity of interaction as well as through the inability to focus on the child" (p. 472). More specifically, depressed mothers tend to be more irritable, withdrawn, emotionally unavailable, and inconsistent in their parenting (Beardslee & Wheelock, 1994). Parents' affective states may contribute to their reports of internalizing behavior as well as the actual occurrence of these behaviors. Manassis and Hood (1998) determined that depressed parents may attend more to the behavioral components of their children's problems than they attend to the affective parts. Secondly, depressed and anxious parents may have difficulty enforcing limits with their children, prompting subjective overestimates of conduct problems. Further, depressed parents also tend to get into more power struggles over youngsters' behavior which will increase conduct problems. Depressed parents are less likely to constructively resolve interpersonal conflicts (Beardslee & Wheelock, 1994).

A parent's perceptions of their children's fears play an important role in referral patterns. Beidel, Silverman, and Hammond-Laurence (1996) concluded that parents who see the anxiety as troubling for their children are more likely to take their children to a mental health professional, whereas parents with a high tolerance for anxiety will be less likely to consult a mental health professional. Children whose parents are less attuned to their youngsters' anxious inner experiences may be less likely to receive services.

Information regarding parental anxiety, depression, or other psychological disturbances has several clinical implications (Kendall et al., 1991). If parental psychopathology is present, clinicians must consider whether a referral for individual treatment for the parent is necessary. Secondly, therapists must design a treatment plan for the child that mindfully considers parental level of distress. For example, the coping skills training is based on a transfer of control model (Silverman & Kurtines, 1996). According to this model, children have difficulty regulating their moods. They learn self-control through parents, teachers, and therapists. Frequently, therapists will train parents in methods to facilitate greater self-control in their children. However, for parents who themselves suffer self-control deficits, parent training becomes more complicated.

## SUGGESTIONS FOR
## WORKING WITH PARENTS

We offer several recommendations based on our clinical experience and the extant literature (Kendall et al., 1991; Silverman & Kurtines, 1996). First, parental self-control deficits could become a focus of a child's treatment. Therapists could center on the way the parents' self-control deficits contribute to problems managing the parent-child relationship. Secondly, the self-control problems could bring a referral for parents' individual treatment. Thirdly, if the therapist is unable to engage the parent in some treatment approach, self-control skills could still be taught to the child. As the child improves their self-regulation, there will be less stress in the family. The parent may indirectly experience improvements in self-control, and consequently the parent may feel more efficacious.

Kendall et al. (1991) noted that parents of anxious children may be either underinvolved or overprotective. Underinvolved parents may have difficulty keeping appointments, following through with contingency contracts, and promoting children's in-session work at home and school. Clearly, therapists need to increase parental involvement in treatment. Lack of involvement needs to be addressed directly. With extremely underinvolved parents, therapists may need to adopt a graduated approach. For instance, regular contact could be initially established via the telephone. After success with telephone contact, therapists might see parents at the end of each session. As parents become more comfortable, the length of parental sessions could be gradually increased.

At the other end of the involvement continuum, there is the challenge of overprotective parents (Kendall et al., 1991). Examining parental beliefs can be a robust clinical strategy. Kendall and his colleagues astutely point out that these parents may equate being a good parent with being always needed. Thus, a child's movement toward independence and competence is perceived as threatening. Chorpita and Barlow (1998) defined overprotection as "excessive parental involvement in controlling the child's environment to minimize aversive experiences for the child" (p. 12). The therapist should treat this dynamic issue gingerly to avoid premature terminations. Providing parents with information regarding treatment plans and progress is vital. Moreover, helping parents modify their beliefs that being a "good parent means you are always needed" is a productive strategy. Therapists might ask parents, "What else defines good parenting other than always being needed by your child?"

Guilt is another issue in parental work. "The stress of dealing with an anxious child," Kendall et al. (1991) wrote, "may lead parents to become sensitized to any signs of anxiety in their children. They may be hypervigilant and strongly react to any indication of anxiety" (p.156). Not astonishingly, many parents experience a sort of emotional perfectionism. They expect their child not to have any signs of distress. Consequently, when the child may become understandably anxious or depressed about a negative event (e.g., grade on a test, peer rejection), the hypervigilant parent becomes unduly alarmed.

Parents should also be reminded about the high probability of therapeutic lapse and relapse. In our experiences, both children and their parents appreciate gaining an understanding that therapeutic progress is rarely linear. There will be normal ups and downs in their children's skill acquisition and application. Realizing that problems are expected and that change rarely occurs without challenge helps families tolerate lapses in progress.

In our clinical experiences, lapses become especially distressing to parents and children who have emotional perfectionism. For these individuals, they expect to experience no distress, and any negative feelings are seen as flaws. Further, they believe treatment will extinguish negative emotions such as sadness or anxiety rather than modulate these internal states. Emotionally perfectionistic parents may see relatively normal bursts of anxiety and depression as problematic.

Children will, of course, experience stressors and react emotionally to them. For instance, a child may come home naturally upset after a rough day at school where they did poorly on a test and had a nasty argument with a friend. In these instances, parents need to remember that children are being taught coping skills rather than ways to eliminate all negative emotional experiences.

Helping parents identify the ways their children recover from normal, unpleasant experiences can attenuate emotional perfectionism. Instead of viewing progress as an all-or-nothing phenomenon, parents can learn to conceptualize progress from a relativistic position. Learning to compare the frequency, intensity, and duration of children's negative emotions during and after treatment to pretreatment levels can be a very useful strategy. Naturally, children should experience distressing feelings more infrequently, less intensely, and for shorter periods after treatment. These indices reflect children's capacity to recover from inevitable upsets and accordingly represent better barometers of change rather than the absence of negative moods.

Talking with parents about the nature of anxiety and depression is a first step in parent education (Kendall et al., 1991). Parents can be presented with information on the prevalence, symptoms, risk factors, and course of these disorders. Many parents may find this information reassuring and normalizing. Often, this educational information may stimulate further discussion and lay the groundwork for subsequent parental interventions. Therapists may wish to connect symptom presentation to treatment strategies. In this way, educational information and treatment rationale are simultaneously being explained. Discussing the course of treatment and explicating parental expectations are also productive options. Knowing that they should not initially expect dramatic changes is helpful for parents. Accordingly, they can form more realistic expectations of progress. Attention can be directed to the small, graduated gains children make. With increased parental attention and reinforcement to these graduated steps, the frequency of overall positive reinforcement will increase. Consequently, these small improvements promote momentum and greater progress.

Providing parents with appropriate expectations regarding children's emotional functioning can be very reassuring to parents. Moreover, helping parents become more developmentally sensitive may attenuate problems (Kendall et al., 1991). Vernon and Al-Mabuk's (1995) parenting book, *What Growing Up Is All About: A Parent's Guide to Child and Adolescent Development*, offers some very handy developmental material.

### Providing Feedback

Providing feedback to parents is a practical and potentially impactful way to educate parents. Feedback regarding children's progress may be given informally as well as formally. In the PANDY Program conducted at the Wright State University School of Professional Psychology, we frequently gave graphs to parents depicting children's progress in the program. We gave children the Children's Depression Inventory (CDI; Kovacs, 1992) and the Revised Children's Manifest Anxiety Scale (RCMAS; Reynolds & Richmond, 1985) at regular intervals. The T-scores and scaled scores were plotted and given to the parents as a concrete record of progress. Similarly, parents can be given formal, concrete feedback on children's completion of assignments in *Therapeutic Exercises for Children*. For instance, the *Memory Jogger* worksheet could serve as a form of feedback. Additionally, parents could be told which specific skills the child has acquired and applied.

Feedback can also be much less formal. In our clinic-based PANDY Program, we met with parents at the end of each group. During this time, children were invited to share with their parents whatever they wished about the group. Group therapists told the parents about skills and techniques presented that week in group. Moreover, during specific parent groups, we discussed parents' perceptions of children's progress and provided educational information.

Including parents in treatment as contingency managers is a strategy recommended by many cognitive-behavioral therapists (Kendall et al., 1991; Silverman & Kurtines, 1996). Parents can be taught rudimentary behavioral principles such as goal setting, contracting, shaping, and contingent rewards. In our PANDY Program, we often provide didactic material to parents such as mini-lectures and educational handouts. We rely on the excellent work by Becker (1977), Forehand and McMahon (1981), Patterson (1976), and Vernon and Al-Mabuk (1995).

Providing parents with handy reading material is also a productive practice. We routinely give parents whose children are in our clinic-based PANDY Program Seligman et al.'s (1995) parenting book, *The Optimistic Child*. *The Optimistic Child* is a nice accompaniment for parents to *Therapeutic Exercises for Children* since they share the theoretical basis for skills children learn.

## CONCLUSION

Placing *Therapeutic Exercises for Children* in a familial context is a critical yet formidable task. The greater the family involvement, the more portable the skills become. Parental involvement may be moderated by levels of psychopathology, marital conflict, or parenting skills deficits. Therapists are challenged to devise creative means to engage parents in work with *Therapeutic Exercises for Children*. Sharing the exercises and rationale behind them are gainful therapeutic strategies. Providing regular feedback to parents is an important way to enlist cooperation. Resource material also supports parenting efforts. The skills in *Therapeutic Exercises for Children* will be greatly enhanced by therapists who mindfully address these issues.

# CHAPTER 9

# Issues in School-Based Applications of *Therapeutic Exercises for Children*

## INTRODUCTION

The current literature discusses the gap between the needs of youth and existing mental health programs (B. J. Burns & Friedman, 1990; Duchnowski & Friedman, 1990; Kelleher, Taylor, & Rickert, 1992; Knitzer, 1982; Weist, 1997). Traditional barriers such as transportation, the stigma associated with mental health, familial stress, financial issues, and lack of knowledge about services often prevent many families from receiving adequate care (Weist, 1997). In an attempt to increase the likelihood that services reach children in need, educators, therapists, and physicians have joined forces to advocate that health and mental health services be expanded to schools. Offering mental health programs in schools serves to lessen barriers and increase access to needed services (Weist, 1997).

Utilizing the *Therapeutic Exercises for Children* materials with a group of youth in a school setting will pose a challenge for even the most experienced therapists. The school setting brings inherent characteristics that may represent obstacles to effective implementation. School systems operate in very different ways from mental health systems. As Waxman, Weist, and Benson (1999) aptly noted, "Teachers' perceptions are shaped by their experiences with children whose behavior is consistent with developmental norms, whereas mental health clinicians typically work with children who are having problems that set them apart from norms" (p. 243). Determining whom to approach within the school setting can be difficult. The program and materials may have to be approved by school administration, which may slow down the process. Often, schools do not have the funds to finance out-side programs. Thus, alternative sources of funding must be located and utilized. Further, the program must be integrated into an already busy school schedule. To achieve this, program personnel often have to be extremely flexible. Ongoing communication with parents can be difficult because parents are not bringing the children to the group. In addition, parents may not have the same financial investment they would if the group was clinic-based. Accordingly, parents may decrease their motivation for active participation. Finally, balancing student confidentiality against open communication with teachers and other school personnel is one of the most challenging aspects of working within a school system (Waxman et al., 1999).

## ADVANTAGES OF
## SCHOOL-BASED GROUPS

There are distinct advantages to using *Therapeutic Exercises for Children* in school-based groups. First, transportation, financial, and environmental barriers may be reduced, thereby increasing group at-tendance (Weist, 1997). In clinic-based groups, transportation diffi-culties account for a high number of missed or canceled appointments. In contrast, families tend to have a routine way of getting their child to school whether by walking, riding the bus, or car-pooling. This lessens the chances that a child will miss a group session due to transportation issues. Parents are not usually required to pay for their child to partici-pate in school groups. Thus, the financial burden of many clinic-based groups is removed. Weather-related cancellations may also be reduced. Clinic-based groups tend to be offered in the evening while school-based groups occur during the day. Families may be more likely to drive in bad weather during the day than they are to leave their homes at night.

A second advantage to conducting school-based groups is that the school is an environment that already promotes learning. Children at-tend classes to acquire new facts and develop new skills on a daily basis. Thus, attending a group in which they are taught cognitive-behavioral strategies to reduce their anxious and depressive thoughts seems commonplace. In fact, children may even view the group as a special kind of class.

Conducting a group in a school setting also reduces some of the anxiety that comes with attending a clinic-based group. In a school setting, some of the children may already know each other. In addition, the surroundings are familiar. Children may worry less about what the other children in the group will be like because they know they will be fellow students. Moreover, all group members start out with one thing in common: they attend the same school!

A fourth advantage to school-based groups is that the location may reduce the stigma that is frequently associated with seeking mental health services from a community agency or private practitioner (Weist, 1997). Referred children do not have to enter a mental health agency. Instead, they receive services in a natural environment (Weist, 1997). They also do not have to worry about other youngsters seeing them at the facility or finding out that they are receiving mental health services. If the group can be integrated into the school as an activity, the stigma may be reduced even further. For example, we refer to our school-based groups as the "PANDY Club." The PANDY Club is viewed as a desirable extracurricular school program. The idea of referring to the program as a "Club" was borrowed from the Positive Adolescent Choices Training (PACT) Program, a school-based violence prevention program developed at Wright State University by Yung and Hammond (1995). The Club is described as a place to have fun, meet other kids, and practice ways to feel better about yourself as well as get along better with others. This strategy appears to work very well, as students who are not members of the Club will spontaneously ask group leaders if they can become members.

Further, the support of school personnel and parents promotes generalization of skills in two settings: home and school. With clinic-based groups, parents are often taught to reinforce skills at home. The advantage of school-based groups is that teachers and school personnel can also be taught to reinforce target skills. The school then becomes another environment where children can practice skills and receive feedback.

The last advantage to conducting groups in schools is that it provides more flexibility in terms of scheduling. It is very easy to schedule two groups per week. Parents may have difficulties transporting children to a community-based clinic twice a week. Also, children may have conflicting practices for sports or other activities on some evenings. These barriers are removed with school-based groups. In addition, conducting a group in the school offers an opportunity to integrate the group into an existing schedule. For example, groups can be run for one quarter, two quarters, or an entire year. Once a set time and day are established, the school-based group becomes a part of the regular school schedule.

It is clear that school-based groups have several advantages over clinic-based groups. The location reduces common barriers, such as stigma and transportation, that keep families from accessing services. In addition, training school personnel to reinforce target skills promotes generalization of skills outside the home setting. The familiarity of the school environment also serves to reduce the stigma of receiving services and reinforces the learning focus. Flexibility of scheduling is another advantage since programs can become a part of the regular school schedule. Thus, although the implementation of a group in a school setting may be a challenge, we highly recommend it. The advantages clearly outweigh the challenges. With careful planning and consideration, a school-based group that uses *Therapeutic Exercises for Children* can be a very successful endeavor. Accordingly, this chapter will discuss suggestions for initiating a school-based group.

## GENERAL CONSIDERATIONS

This section will discuss general issues to be considered in moving from the planning stages to the implementation of an actual school-based group. First, program personnel must select an appropriate school. Although this appears to be a relatively simple task, school selection may represent a frustrating and time-consuming step. Second, program planners must attain administrative and financial support from the designated school. Third, program personnel must decide how information will be shared with school personnel, parents, and students. Fourth, program planners should anticipate what school and program adaptations are necessary for successful implementation.

### The School Selection Process

*Selecting a School.* There are three main issues that make the school selection process a challenge: (a) the way schools select and approve mental health-related programs, (b) preexisting relationships with mental health agencies, and (c) the allocation of school resources. School districts handle the issue of program selection and approval in different ways. Some school districts have central offices or boards that must approve all school-related health or mental health services. Other school districts operate relatively independently. That is, each school can select its own programs. Still other school districts utilize a combined approach in that each school has the ability to select a limited number of health- or mental health-related programs. It is important to research particular school districts to determine requirements for program entry into the system. Consultation with the local school board and other professionals who operate programs within the school district is key.

School districts may have preexisting relationships with other agencies for mental health services. As a result, they may be reluctant to begin a new relationship. One way to address this issue is increasing awareness of these preexisting relationships and describing the program as an addition to existing services or a program that will reach a new group of students.

Generally, school districts choose to allocate resources based on their philosophy about education. Some school districts have broadly defined educational missions which include providing health and mental health services to students. The thinking is that these services enrich education and allow students to achieve at their optimal level because physical and psychosocial barriers to learning are removed. Other school districts have psychosocial needs but choose to spend all their financial and programmatic resources on educational needs (Weist, 1997). These school districts believe that education is the first and only priority for schools. Mental health services are viewed as beyond the extent of the educational mission. Establishing a program in a school district with the latter philosophy would be a formidable challenge.

With adequate preparation and a little persistence, these issues can be navigated successfully and an appropriate school selected. The task is to identify a school within the district that has the desired population and school personnel who are interested and motivated to make the program successful. The amount and variety of programs that already exist within a particular school should guide the decision-making process. For example, if a school has a number of programs for children with a variety of needs (e.g., anger management, social skills, and conflict resolution), a program for depressed and anxious youngsters could easily get overlooked. The demands of balancing so many programs may result in school personnel being less cognizant of the program's needs. On the other hand, if a school has no outside programs, establishing a program will require much time and effort. The school will not have previous experience to draw upon and will be required to make adaptations for the first time. Logistical problems often arise and may impede program implementation. We recommend selecting a school with one or two existing programs. This type of school tends to quickly adjust to the needs of an outside program and school personnel will be motivated to assist with program activities.

There are several signs that indicate an appropriate school has been selected. First, the school will understand the importance of identifying and providing services to children with internalizing problems. Second, school personnel will encourage communication (i.e., return phone calls, ask questions) and agree to schedule an in-service for teachers. Schools committed to having the program will typically provide a designated contact person, provide dedicated space, and offer the use of equipment.

## Approaching the School

It is important to identify an initial contact person at the school. Although you will need to work closely with the school counselor to initiate referrals and follow-up with teachers, the school counselor may not be the best person to contact. Finding the person responsible for helping the school secure resources is an important goal. This person should be the initial contact. A simple phone call to the school secretary may be all it takes to obtain this information.

## Meeting With School Personnel

The next step is scheduling a meeting with the contact person during which an overview of the program is provided. The presentation should include information about anxiety and depression in youth, theoretical foundations for the *Therapeutic Exercises for Children* program, a program description, intervention methods, and program evaluation procedures. The presentation should also include data regarding the number of students to be served by the program, types of services offered, plans for referring students who are not appropriate, and any financial constraints. Anticipating questions from school personnel such as "How will we know the program is effective?" "What type of communication can we expect from the program?" and "What must the school contribute to the program?" will facilitate a productive meeting. Finally, sharing data on the success of the program and providing the school with references are compelling strategies.

Conducting an in-service for teachers and other school personnel serves several important functions (R. D. Friedberg et al., 1998; Waxman et al., 1999). First, presentations enhance relationships with school personnel (Waxman et al., 1999). Secondly, these in-service training opportunities provide valuable information at no cost to the school. Demonstrating empathy for school personnel is a fundamental consultative task (Bostic & Rauch, 1999). Accordingly, presentations provide a wonderful opportunity to demonstrate an understanding of the demands placed upon school personnel.

Educating the school personnel will help them become better referral sources. We recommend that program planners devote considerable time teaching school personnel to identify the most appropriate children for the program. In the PANDY Program, we developed a checklist (below) for teachers as a handy guide. It illustrates the criteria we have found helpful in helping identify children for the program.

---

### CHECKLIST FOR REFERRALS TO THE PANDY PROGRAM

Criteria for Inclusion (check as many as apply)

- ☐ Sad mood
- ☐ Irritable mood
- ☐ Edginess
- ☐ Pessimistic
- ☐ Seems not to have fun
- ☐ Sullen
- ☐ Lonely
- ☐ Withdrawn
- ☐ Complies with teacher commands and requests
- ☐ Fear of failure
- ☐ Respects rules and teacher authority

- ☐ Very shy
- ☐ Asks to go to the nurse a lot
- ☐ Fears criticism
- ☐ Needs a lot of reassurance
- ☐ Worries a lot
- ☐ Reads and comprehends at an 8-year-old level
- ☐ Avoids doing schoolwork due to fears of making a mistake
- ☐ Pays attention fairly well
- ☐ Keeps hands and feet to himself/herself

Exclusion Criteria (need only one to exclude)

- ☐ Reading level below 8-year-old level
- ☐ Active thoughts of harming self and/or others
- ☐ Destroys own property and/or the property of others
- ☐ Disobedient, disrupts classroom

- ☐ Violent behavior (attacks school staff or peers)
- ☐ Constant refusal to follow instructions
- ☐ Attempts to hurt self
- ☐ Inattentive

---

### The Implementation Plan

The final step in the selection process is developing an implementation plan. Most schools appreciate a written document which delineates the plan. Beginning the implementation plan with a brief theoretical and empirical rationale places the program in context. The implementation plan should outline referral, intake, selection, parental permission, and intervention processes (Waxman et al., 1999). Moreover, agreements about time, location, and funding should be defined. Providing the names of group leaders is also quite helpful.

## OBTAINING SCHOOL SUPPORT

### Garnering Commitment

A successful program is dependent upon the support of school administration and other personnel. One of the ways to obtain this support is ensuring that the goals of the program are consistent with the school's mission. Demonstrating how coping with anxiety and depression improves children's academic performance is a good idea. Additionally, *Therapeutic Exercises for Children* helps increase children's social skills and their ability to get along with other children in a learning environment. Referring children involved in the program to other school services may be another way to garner support. This referral process reflects a cooperative attitude and a willingness to work with all school personnel. In addition, a program should have access to outside resources for students who are not appropriate for the program's services. This system indicates a caring attitude and communicates a willingness to find resources for students.

Flexibility is important for obtaining school commitment. A willingness to adapt your program as needed to fit within the school's culture goes a long way toward productive school relations (Waxman et al., 1999). More specific information about adaptations will be provided in the next section. Keeping open communication with the contact person and school administration will also facilitate a supportive relationship. Issues that arise should be brought to the attention of school personnel immediately. The goal should be to work out a solution, not complain about a problematic situation.

Finally, getting the school to make a financial contribution to the program increases the school's investment. The school has already agreed to provide space and equipment. Asking the school to contribute incentives or pay for the celebration at the conclusion of the group may increase the school's motivation to make the program a success. Obtaining school commitment is vital for ensuring the cooperation of other school personnel, parents, and students.

## Methods of Communication

Communication is a key variable in program success. It is important to consider when, how, and what will be communicated to teachers, parents, students, and other school personnel. Group leaders may be placed in the dilemma of protecting the student's confidentiality while maintaining open communication with teachers (Waxman et al., 1999).

## Memos

Memos increase program visibility and provide school personnel and students with an easy way of identifying program correspondence. Memos can be sent to teachers, students, or other school personnel. Therapists might consider sending a memo to teachers thanking them for their help in the referral process. A separate memo could provide them with the names of group members, as well as the day, time, and location of group sessions. Thus, classroom teachers will know which children to excuse from their classroom. Correspondence to teachers should always include the names and numbers of group facilitators and the school contact person. At the close of the program, we suggest sending a memo to teachers thanking them for their continued support and providing them with some information about group members' perceptions of the program (with parental consent and child assent, of course). Teachers appreciate feedback on students. It increases the likelihood that they will refer another student in the future and support a school-based program.

Memos work well for students, too. Sending individualized memos congratulating students on becoming members of the program is a nice way of building a relationship prior to initiating group sessions. When youngsters attend the first session, it is a good idea to give them a welcome memo reminding them of the day and time of sessions. Memos may be a useful way to remind them of mousework assignments. Memos can also be used to inform students of cancellations or other schedule changes.

## Communication With Parents

Facilitating communication with parents may be more difficult in school-based groups. In clinic-based groups, there is ongoing contact with parents because they bring their children to the group. If group leaders have concerns about a particular child or want to check on a specific behavior, they have weekly opportunities to do so. This may not be the case with school-based groups.

The intake session is the first opportunity for communication with parents. The extent of parental involvement should be clearly outlined at this stage. Parents will need to attend parent meetings, follow-up sessions, and complete necessary paperwork. Group leaders should collect specifics about the best way to reach parents. Likewise, parents should be given the names and numbers of group leaders as well as the best way to contact them. We recommend checking parent availability for upcoming parent meetings during this session. This will simplify the process of scheduling parent sessions.

When communicating with parents, active listening skills are required. Parents need to feel that professionals understand their point of view and wish to help their child. Parents should be encouraged to reinforce concepts covered in the group. In addition, group leaders should help parents focus on strengths and reframe behavior in terms of coping strategies. Parents could also be instructed in basic behavior management skills and ways to increase their children's adaptive internal dialogues.

## Communication With the School

The group should be clearly defined and presented to school personnel. The purpose and focus of the group needs to be unambiguously discussed. In this way, everyone hears the same message. Teachers, parents, and children understand why children are selected for the group, and are able to develop realistic expectations for participation.

Sharing information about students can be a source of tension between school personnel and mental health personnel. Teachers are accustomed to sharing information about youngsters with a wide array of professionals whereas mental health professionals are used to exchanging information with a limited set of people (Waxman et al., 1999). The limits of confidentiality should be clearly stated to school officials, parents, and children. In this way, boundaries can be clearly delineated. Accordingly, group leaders should be careful to share information that is agreed upon by parents and children through a consent form. The interested reader is referred to an article by Gensheimer, Ayers, and Roosa (1993) for additional resource information on confidentiality and ethics in school-based programs.

Teachers and school officials deserve regular progress reports. General information regarding which skills are being taught and how well the group as a whole is acquiring these skills can be shared. This type of general information where no names are associated with the reports respects confidentiality. Teachers will appreciate guidance regarding how they may use *Therapeutic Exercises for Children* skills. In this way, they can help youngsters transport the skills learned in the group to the classroom.

## PARTICIPATION ISSUES

Obtaining parent and child permission is of course a requisite for participation in the program. In the PANDY Program, our approach to consent is multitiered. Teachers gave the school counselor all the referrals. Following this referral, the school counselor contacted the parent or parents providing them with information about the program and intake process. At this point, parents were asked to return a consent form granting program personnel permission to contact them. If the parents consented, the school counselor referred the child to the program. If the parents did not consent or did not return the letter, no further action was taken. Thus, no names were released to the program personnel unless parental consent was assured.

At the initial interview parents and children were asked to complete a consent for treatment form. This consent included information on the program, personnel, limits of confidentiality, telephone calls, correspondence, appointments, scheduling, and access to records. If a child or parent did not consent to treatment at this point, their involvement was terminated.

## ADAPTING
## *THERAPEUTIC EXERCISES FOR CHILDREN*
## TO THE SCHOOL

### School Adaptations

The school will need to make several adaptations in order to make the program work (Waxman et al., 1999). School personnel must be willing to dedicate space to the program for group sessions and intakes. This is sometimes a challenge for schools who barely have enough room to accommodate students. On an administrative level, school personnel must decide how missed classroom time will impact student grades. Within the classroom, teachers must make arrangements with students to complete missed assignments or tests. In addition, teachers must set aside time for completing referral forms. The contact person will need to devote a significant amount of time to securing space and equipment, contacting teachers and parents, communicating with group leaders and school administrators, procuring school financial support, and attending to program needs.

### Integrating the Program into the School's Culture

Mental health professionals are well-advised to make accommodations so their programs can be assimilated into the school's culture (Waxman et al., 1999; Weist, 1997). Integrating the group into the existing culture of the school can be a challenge because groups must be scheduled at times that meet school needs. Some schools prefer that children attend group sessions in lieu of their general education classes (e.g., reading, math, and spelling). The thinking is that it will be easier to make up work since classes are offered each day. Other schools prefer to take children out of special classes (e.g., art or music). In these circumstances, these schools believe that the children should not miss core educational classes. Group sessions must also be scheduled around regularly occurring school activities, holidays, breaks, and other scheduled activities such as field trips. Group leaders must be flexible and understand that conflicting activities may arise at the last moment. Group sessions may have to be canceled, rescheduled, or postponed.

### CONDUCTING THE GROUP

### Group Content, Process, and Composition

Agenda setting for school-based groups should follow the principles discussed in Chapters 4 and 7. However, in our experience, school-based groups tend to be shorter than clinic-based groups. Schools generally do not want their youngsters removed from their daily academic routine for more than 45 minutes. Thus, group leaders need to be quite focused and emphasize skills that match the children's problems. All the *Therapeutic Exercises for Children* skills are suitable for school-based groups.

Considerations for group process are similar in school-based and clinic-based groups. Chapter 7 delineates several recommendations for group process. It is important for group leaders to help children acquire and apply the skills. Additionally, group leaders should diligently help children cope with emotional issues within the group. In our clinical experience, helping the children resolve the issue in the group rather than allowing anyone to leave group and return to the class in a distressed state is a productive strategy. In this way, a boundary is delineated between schoolwork and therapy. Moreover, the child's performance in class is not adversely affected by the issues generated in the group. Parents, teachers, and the children seem to appreciate this strategy.

Group composition issues were discussed in Chapter 7. The recommendations discussed in Chapter 7 also held true for school-based groups. Flexibility and therapeutic sensitivity are necessary to manage group composition issues.

### School Suicide Intervention Protocol

Suicidal ideation is common when working with depressed youngsters. Accordingly, therapists working in a school-based program need to be cognizant of the suicide intervention protocol established by the school. Typically, this involves notifying the school counselor who will follow appropriate school procedure. Thus, discussing this issue with the school counselor prior to starting the group facilitates proper handling of the situation and avoids mishaps. The school will likely have an established method for managing these crises and therapists need to be familiar with school procedures. In the rare circumstance where procedures are not established, therapists are well-advised to work with the school to develop an appropriate protocol.

### Student Illness or Injury Policy

Although the probability for student illness or injury during a group is relatively low, therapists need to be familiar with the school procedures for injury and illness. Generally, the protocol involves informing the school nurse or main office staff. For example, one child in the PANDY groups complained of acute shortness of breath during a session. The child was taken to the office where school personnel observed him until he felt better. Before returning to the group, he was evaluated by the school nurse. Clarifying these issues with school personnel prior to conducting group sessions is time well spent. Ensuring that each group member has an emergency notification form on file is a good policy.

## Staffing Considerations

Ideally, experienced counselors or therapists will lead the groups. With inexperienced therapists, proper supervision is indicated. Training in group processes and group behavior management is essential. Group leaders should be familiar with the issues challenging school-based intervention programs. More specifically, they should receive training in confidentiality issues and school policies (Hallfors et al., 1996). Yung and Hammond (1995) suggest that group leaders possess the following personal qualities: "Committed and enthusiastic, confident and assertive, observant and decisive, supportive and reinforcing, patient and tenacious, attentive and perceptive, creative and persuasive, flexible and resourceful" (p. 29).

Effective school group leaders understand the need for flexibility and the importance of maintaining rapport with school officials. Moreover, they should be team players who can work collaboratively with school personnel. This collaboration requires frequent contact with school personnel. Additionally, group leaders must consider that the program needs may not be the school's first priority at all times.

## CONCLUSION

Adapting *Therapeutic Exercises for Children* for school use is a complex and challenging task. Nonetheless, school-based groups offer considerable advantages to children and clinicians. Various obstacles can be overcome and multiple benefits can be realized. Solid and vibrant teamwork between mental health and school professionals is a rewarding experience. Modifying *Therapeutic Exercises for Children* for the school setting and including it as part of an emotional curriculum is an exciting clinical frontier.

# References

Abramson, L. Y., Seligman, M. E. P., & Teasdale, J. D. (1978). Learned helplessness in humans: Critique and reformulation. *Journal of Abnormal Psychology, 87,* 49-74.

Albano, A. M., & Barlow, D. H. (1996). Breaking the vicious cycle: Cognitive-behavioral group treatment for anxious youth. In E. D. Hibbs & P. S. Jensen (Eds.), *Psychosocial Treatments for Child and Adolescent Disorders: Empirically-Based Strategies for Clinical Practice* (pp. 23-42). Washington, DC: American Psychological Association.

Albano, A. M., & DiBartolo, P. M. (1997). Cognitive-behavioral treatment of obsessive-compulsive disorder and social phobia in children and adolescents. In L. Vandecreek, S. Knapp, & T. L. Jackson (Eds.), *Innovations in Clinical Practice: A Source Book* (Vol. 15, pp. 41-58). Sarasota, FL: Professional Resource Press.

Alford, B. A., & Beck, A. T. (1997). *The Integrative Power of Cognitive Therapy.* New York: Guilford.

Allen, J. (1998). Personality assessment with American Indians and Alaska Natives: Instrument considerations and service delivery style. *Journal of Personality Assessment, 70,* 17-42.

American Academy of Child and Adolescent Psychiatry. (1997). Practice parameters for the assessment and treatment of children and adolescents with anxiety disorders. *Journal of the American Academy of Child and Adolescent Psychiatry, 36,* 69-84.

American Psychiatric Association. (1994). *Diagnostic and Statistical Manual of Mental Disorders* (4th ed.). Washington, DC: Author.

Bandura, A. (1977a). Self-efficacy: Toward a unifying theory of behavior change. *Psychological Review, 84,* 191-215.

Bandura, A. (1977b). *Social Learning Theory.* Englewood Cliffs, NJ: Prentice-Hall.

Bandura, A. (1986). *Social Foundations of Thought and Action.* Englewood Cliffs, NJ: Prentice-Hall.

Barlow, D. H. (1993). *Clinical Handbook of Adult Disorders.* New York: Guilford.

Beardslee, W. R., Salt, P., Porterfield, K., Rothberg, P. C., Vandeveld, P., Swatling, S., Hoke, L., Moilanen, D. L., & Wheelock, I. (1993). Comparison of preventive interventions for families with parental affective disorder. *Journal of the American Academy of Child and Adolescent Psychiatry, 32,* 254-263.

Beardslee, W. R., & Wheelock, I. (1994). Children of parents with affective disorders: Empirical findings and clinical implications. In W. M. Reynolds & H. F. Johnston (Eds.), *Handbook of Depression in Children and Adolescents* (pp. 463-479). New York: Plenum.

Beardslee, W. R., Wright, E. J., Salt, P., Drezner, K., Gladstone, T. R. G., Versage, E. M., & Rothberg, P. C. (1997). Examination of children's responses to two preventive intervention strategies over time. *Journal of the American Academy of Child and Adolescent Psychiatry, 36,* 196-204.

Beck, A. T. (1976). *Cognitive Therapy and the Emotional Disorders.* New York: International Universities Press.

Beck, A. T. (1985). Cognitive therapy, behavior therapy, psychoanalysis, and pharmacotherapy: A cognitive continuum. In M. J. Mahoney & A. Freeman (Eds.), *Cognition and Psychotherapy* (pp. 325-347). New York: Plenum.

Beck, A. T., & Clark, D. A. (1998). Anxiety and depression: An information processing perspective. *Anxiety Research: An International Journal, 1,* 23-36.

Beck, A. T., Emery, G., & Greenberg, R. L. (1985). *Anxiety Disorders and Phobias: A Cognitive Perspective.* New York: Plenum.

Beck, A. T., Rush, A. J., Shaw, B. F., & Emery, G. (1979). *Cognitive Therapy of Depression.* New York: Guilford.

Beck, J. S. (1995). *Cognitive Therapy: Basics and Beyond.* New York: Guilford.

Becker, W. C. (1977). *Parents Are Teachers: A Child Management Program.* Champaign, IL: Research Press.

Beidel, D. C., Fink, C. M., & Turner, S. M. (1996). Stability of anxious symptomatology in children. *Journal of Abnormal Child Psychology, 24,* 257-269.

Beidel, D. C., & Morris, T. L. (1995). Social phobia. In J. S. March (Ed.), *Anxiety Disorders in Children and Adolescents* (pp. 181-211). New York: Guilford.

Beidel, D. C., Silverman, W. K., & Hammond-Laurence, K. (1996). Overanxious disorder: Subsyndromal state or specific disorder?: A comparison of clinic and community samples. *Journal of Clinical Child Psychology, 25,* 25-32.

Beidel, D. C., Turner, M. W., & Trager, K. N. (1994). Test anxiety and childhood disorders in African-American and white school children. *Journal of Anxiety Disorders, 8,* 169-179.

Beidel, D. C., & Turner, S. M. (1997). At risk for anxiety: Psychopathology in the offspring of anxious parents. *Journal of the American Academy of Child and Adolescent Psychiatry, 36,* 918-924.

Beidel, D. C., & Turner, S. M. (1998). *Shy Children, Phobic Adults.* Washington, DC: American Psychological Association.

Bell-Dolan, D. J., Last, C. G., & Strauss, C. C. (1990). Symptoms of anxiety in normal children. *Journal of the American Academy of Child and Adolescent Psychiatry, 29,* 759-765.

Bell-Dolan, D. J., & Wessler, A. E. (1994). Attributional style of anxious children: Extensions from cognitive theory and research on adult anxiety. *Journal of Anxiety Disorders, 8,* 79-96.

Bernstein, G. A., & Borchardt, C. M. (1991). Anxiety disorders of childhood and adolescence: A critical review. *Journal of the American Academy of Child and Adolescent Psychiatry, 30,* 519-532.

Bernstein, G. A., Borchardt, C. M., & Perwien, A. R. (1996). Anxiety disorders in children and adolescents: A review of the past 10 years. *Journal of the American Academy of Child and Adolescent Psychiatry, 35,* 1110-1119.

Beutler, L. E., Brown, M. T., Crothers, L., Booker, K., & Seabrook, M. K. (1996). The dilemma of factitious demographic distinctions in psychological research. *Journal of Consulting and Clinical Psychology, 64,* 892-902.

Birmaher, B., Ryan, N. D., Williamson, D. E., Brent, D. A., Kaufman, J., Dahl, R. E., Perel, J., & Nelson, B. (1996). Childhood and adolescent depression: A review of the past 10 years: Part I. *Journal of the American Academy of Child and Adolescent Psychiatry, 35,* 1427-1439.

Bostic, J. Q., & Rauch, P. K. (1999). The 3 R's of school consultation. *Journal of the American Academy of Child and Adolescent Psychiatry, 38,* 339-341.

Burns, B. J., & Friedman, R. M. (1990). Examining the research base for child mental health services and policy. *Journal of Mental Health Administration, 17,* 87-97.

Burns, D. D. (1980). *Feeling Good: The New Mood Therapy.* New York: Signet.

Burns, D. D. (1989). *The Feeling Good Handbook.* New York: William Morrow.

Callahan, S. A., Panichelli-Mindel, S. M., & Kendall, P. C. (1996). DSM-IV and internalizing disorders: Modification, limitations, and utility. *School Psychology Review, 25,* 297-307.

Chorpita, B. F., & Barlow, D. H. (1998). The development of anxiety: The role of control in the early environment. *Psychological Bulletin, 124,* 3-21.

Cole, D. A., Martin, J. M., Peeke, A., Henderson, A., & Harwell, J. (1998). Validation of depression and anxiety measures in White and Black youths: Multitrait-multimethod analysis. *Psychological Assessment, 10,* 261-276.

Cole, D. A., Peeke, L. G., Martin, J. M., Truglio, R., & Seroczynski, A. D. (1998). A longitudinal look at the relationship between depression and anxiety in children and adolescents. *Journal of Consulting and Clinical Psychology, 66,* 451-460.

Cole, P. M., & Kaslow, N. J. (1988). Interactional and cognitive strategies for affect regulation: Developmental perspectives on childhood depression. In L. B. Alloy (Ed.), *Cognitive Processes in Depression* (pp. 310-343). New York: Guilford.

Conger, J. C., & Keane, S. P. (1981). Social skills intervention in the treatment of isolated and withdrawn children. *Psychological Bulletin, 90,* 478-495.

Costanzo, P., Miller-Johnson, S., & Wencel, H. (1995). Social development. In J. S. March (Ed.), *Anxiety Disorders in Children and Adolescents* (pp. 82-108). New York: Guilford.

Cuellar, I. (1998). Cross-cultural psychological assessment of Hispanic Americans. *Journal of Personality Assessment, 70,* 71-86.

Curry, J. F., & Murphy, L. B. (1995). Comorbidity of anxiety disorders in children and adolescents. In J. S. March (Ed.), *Anxiety Disorders in Children and Adolescents* (pp. 301-317). New York: Guilford.

Dadds, M. R., Spence, S. H., Holland, D. E., Barrett, P. M., & Laurens, K. R. (1997). Prevention and early intervention for anxiety and disorders: A controlled trial. *Journal of Consulting and Clinical Psychology, 65,* 627-635.

Dana, R. H. (1998). Personality assessment and the cultural self: Emic and etic contexts as learning resources. In L. Handler & M. Hilsenroth (Eds.), *Teaching and Learning Personality Assessment* (pp. 325-346). Mahwah, NJ: Lawrence Erlbaum.

DeRoos, Y., & Allen-Meares, P. (1998). Application of Rasch analysis: Exploring differences in depression between African-American and White children. *Journal of Social Service Research, 23,* 93-107.

Diener, C., & Dweck, C. (1980). An analysis of learned helplessness: The processing of success. *Journal of Personality and Social Psychology, 39,* 940-952.

Dion, R., Gotowiec, A., & Beiser, M. (1998). Depression and conduct disorder in Native and Non-Native children. *Journal of the American Academy of Child and Adolescent Psychiatry, 37,* 736-742.

Dodge, K. A. (1985). Attributional bias in aggressive children. In P. C. Kendall (Ed.), *Advances in Cognitive-Behavioral Research and Therapy* (Vol. 4, pp. 73-110). New York: Academic Press.

Duchnowski, A. J., & Friedman, R. M. (1990). Children's mental health: Challenges for the nineties. *Journal of Mental Health Administration, 17,* 3-12.

Dweck, C. (1981). Social cognitive processes in children's friendships. In S. Asher & J. Gottman (Eds.), *The Development of Children's Friendships* (pp. 322-333). London: Cambridge University Press.

D'Zurilla, T. J. (1986). *Problem-Solving Therapy: A Social Competence Approach to Clinical Intervention.* New York: Springer Publishing.

Eisen, A. R., & Silverman, W. K. (1993). Should I relax or change my thoughts. A preliminary examination of cognitive therapy, relaxation, and their combination with overanxious children. *Journal of Cognitive Psychotherapy, 7,* 265-280.

Epkins, C. C. (1996). Cognitive specificity and affective confounding in social anxiety and dysphoria in children. *Journal of Psychopathology and Behavioral Assessment, 18,* 83-101.

Feindler, E. L., & Ecton, R. B. (1986). *Adolescent Anger Control: Cognitive-Behavioral Techniques.* New York: Pergamon.

Feindler, E. L., & Guttman, J. (1994). Cognitive-behavioral anger control training. In C. W. Lecroy (Ed.), *Handbook of Children and Adolescent Treatment Manuals* (pp. 170-199). New York: Lexington.

Finch, A. J., Nelson, W. M., & Ott, E. S. (1993). *Cognitive Behavioral Procedures With Children and Adolescents: A Practical Guide.* Boston: Allyn & Bacon.

Forehand, R. L., & McMahon, R. J. (1981). *Helping the Non-Compliant Child: A Clinician's Guide to Parent Training.* New York: Guilford.

Freeman, A. (1998, December). *Keynote Address.* Behavioral Healthcare Symposium sponsored by Specialty Health Care of Ohio, Columbus, OH.

Freeman, A., & Dattilio, F. M. (1992). *Comprehensive Casebook of Cognitive Therapy.* New York: Plenum.

Freeman, A., Pretzer, J., Fleming, B., & Simon, K. (1990). *Clinical Applications of Cognitive Therapy.* New York: Plenum.

Friedberg, R. D. (1996a). Cognitive-behavioral games and workbooks: Tips for school counselors. *Elementary School Guidance and Counseling, 31,* 11-20.

Friedberg, R. D. (1996b, April). *Cognitive Conundrums: When Therapy Fails.* Daylong workshop presented for Commonwealth Educational Seminars, Burlington, MA.

Friedberg, R. D., Crosby, L. E., Friedberg, B. A., Rutter, J. G., & Knight, K. R. (1999). Making cognitive-behavior therapy user-friendly for children. *Cognitive and Behavioral Practice, 6,* 189-200.

Friedberg, R. D., Crosby, L. E., Polonia, M., Vriesendorp, P., Finney, K., Anderson, L., & Friedberg, B. A. (1998, November). Educating school and medical personnel about depression and anxiety in children. In R. D. Friedberg (Chairperson), *Promising Directions in Medical and School Consultations.* Symposium presentation delivered at the annual meeting of the Association for the Advancement of Behavior Therapy, Washington, DC.

Gensheimer, L. K., Ayers, T. S., & Roosa, M. W. (1993). School-based preventative interventions for at-risk populations: Practical and ethical issues. *Evaluation and Program Planning, 16,* 159-167.

Gillham, J. E., Reivich, K. J., Jaycox, L. H., & Seligman, M. E. P. (1995). Prevention of depressive symptoms in school children. *Psychological Science, 6,* 343-351.

Ginsburg, G. S., La Greca, A. M., & Silverman, W. K. (1998). Social anxiety in children with anxiety disorders: Relation with social and emotional functioning. *Journal of Abnormal Child Psychology, 26,* 175-185.

Ginsburg, G. S., & Silverman, W. K. (1996). Phobic and anxiety disorders in Hispanic and Caucasian youth. *Journal of Anxiety Disorders, 10,* 517-528.

Ginsburg, G. S., Silverman, W. K., & Kurtines, W. S. (1995). Cognitive-behavioral group therapy. In A. R. Eisen, C. A. Kearney, & C. E. Schaefer (Eds.), *Clinical Handbook of Anxiety Disorders in Children and Adolescents* (pp. 521-549). Northvale, NJ: Jason Aronson.

Gladstone, T. R. G., & Kaslow, N. J. (1995). Depression and attributions in children and adolescents: A meta-analytic review. *Journal of Abnormal Child Psychology, 23,* 597-606.

Goldstein, A. P., Glick, B., Reiner, S., Zimmerman, D., & Coultry, T. M. (1987). Aggression replacement training: A comprehensive intervention for aggressive youth. Champaign, IL: Research Press.

Gotlib, I. H., & Hammen, C. L. (1992). *Psychological Aspects of Depression.* New York: John Wiley.

Greenberger, D., & Padesky, C. A. (1995). *Mind Over Mood.* New York: Pergamon.

Hallfors, D., McQuide, P., Braach, C., & Hutcheson, S. (1996). *First Steps: A Guide to Integrating Information for Systems Evaluation of Children's Mental Health Services.* Boston: Judge Baker Children's Center.

Heberlein, W. A., Lonigan, C., & Kistner, J. A. (1997, November). *Common and Unique Variance in the Relationship Between Depression, Anxiety, and Self-Concepts in Children.* Poster presentation at the annual meeting of the Association for the Advancement of Behavior Therapy, Miami, FL.

Hicks, D., Ginsburg, G. S., Lumpkin, P. W., Serafini, L., Bravo, I., Ferguson, C., & Silverman, W. K. (1996, November). *Phobic and Anxiety Disorders in Hispanic and White Youth.* Poster presentation at the annual meeting of the Association for the Advancement of Behavior Therapy, New York, NY.

Ho, M. K. (1992). *Minority Children and Adolescents in Therapy.* Newbury Park, CA: Sage.

Hops, H. (1995). Age and gender-specific effects of parental depression: A commentary. *Developmental Psychology, 31,* 428-431.

Huang, L. N. (1998). Southeast Asian refugee children and adolescents. In J. T. Gibbs & L. N. Huang (Eds.), *Children of Color: Psychological Interventions With Culturally Diverse Youth* (pp. 264-304). San Francisco: Jossey-Bass.

Huang, L. N., & Ying, Y. (1998). Chinese American children and adolescents. In J. T. Gibbs & L. N. Huang (Eds.), *Children of Color: Psychological Interventions With Culturally Diverse Youth* (pp. 33-67). San Francisco: Jossey-Bass.

Jaycox, L. H., Reivich, K. J., Gillham, J. E., & Seligman, M. E. P. (1994). Prevention of depressive symptoms in school children. *Behavior Research and Therapy, 32,* 801-816.

Kashani, J. H., & Orvaschel, H. (1990). A community study of anxiety in children and adolescents. *American Journal of Psychiatry, 147,* 313-318.

Kaslow, N. J., & Rascusin, G. R. (1990). Childhood depression: Current status and future directions. In A. S. Bellack, M. Hersen, & A. E. Kazdin (Eds.), *International Handbook of Behavior Modification and Therapy* (pp. 649-667). New York: Plenum.

Kaslow, N. J., & Thompson, M. P. (1998). Applying the criteria for empirically-supported treatments to studies of psychosocial interventions for child and adolescent depression. *Journal of Clinical Child Psychology, 27,* 146-155.

Kelleher, K. J., Taylor, J. L., & Rickert, V. I. (1992). Mental health services for rural children and adolescents. *Clinical Psychology Review, 12,* 841-852.

Kendall, P. C. (1990). *The Coping Cat Workbook.* Philadelphia: Temple University.

Kendall, P. C. (1992). Childhood coping: Avoiding a lifetime of anxiety. *Behaviour Change, 9,* 229-237.

Kendall, P. C., Chansky, T. E., Friedman, F. M., & Siqueland, L. (1991). Treating anxiety disorders in children and adolescents. In P. C. Kendall (Ed.), *Child and Adolescent Therapy: Cognitive-Behavioral Procedures* (pp. 131-164). New York: Guilford.

Kendall, P. C., Chansky, T. E., Kane, M. T., Kim, R. S., Kortlander, E., Ronan, K. R., Sessa, F. M., & Siqueland, L. (1992). *Anxiety Disorders in Youth: Cognitive-Behavioral Interventions.* Boston: Allyn & Bacon.

Kendall, P. C., MacDonald, J. P., & Treadwell, K. R. H. (1995). The treatment of anxiety disorders in youth. In A. R. Eisen, C. A. Kearney, & C. E. Schaefer (Eds.), *Clinical Handbook of Anxiety Disorders in Children and Adolescents* (pp. 573-597). Northvale, NJ: Jason Aronson.

Kendall, P. C., Panichelli-Mindel, S. M., Sugarman, A., & Callahan, S. A. (1997). Exposure to child anxiety: Theory, research, and practice. *Clinical Psychology: Science and Practice, 4,* 29-39.

Kendall, P. C., & Treadwell, K. R. H. (1996). Cognitive-behavioral treatment for childhood anxiety disorders. In E. D. Hibbs & P. S. Jensen (Eds.), *Psychosocial Treatments for Child and Adolescent Disorders: Empirically-Based Strategies for Clinical Practice* (pp. 23-42). Washington, DC: American Psychological Association.

Klein, R. G., & Last, C. G. (1989). *Anxiety Disorders in Children.* Newbury Park, CA: Sage.

Knell, S. M. (1993). *Cognitive-Behavioral Play Therapy.* Northvale, NJ: Jason Aronson.

Knitzer, J. (1982). *Unclaimed Children: The Failure of Public Responsibility to Children and Adolescents in Need of Mental Health Services.* Washington, DC: Children's Defense Fund.

Kolko, D. S. (1987). Depression. In M. Hersen & V. B. Hasselt (Eds.), *Behavior Therapy With Children and Adolescents* (pp. 137-183). New York: John Wiley.

Koss-Chioino, J. D., & Vargas, L. A. (1992). Through the cultural looking glass: A model for understanding culturally responsive psychotherapies. In L. A. Vargas & J. D. Koss-Chioino (Eds.), *Working With Culture: Psychotherapeutic Interventions With Ethnic Minority Children and Adolescents* (pp. 1-24). San Francisco: Jossey-Bass.

Kovacs, M. (1992). *Children's Depression Inventory.* North Tonawanda, NY: Multi-Health Systems.

Kovacs, M., & Devlin, B. (1998). Internalizing disorders in childhood. *Journal of Child Psychology and Psychiatry, 39,* 47-63.

Kovacs, M., Gatsonis, C., Paulauskas, S. L., & Richards, C. (1989). Depressive disorders in childhood-IV: A longitudinal study of comorbidity with risk for anxiety disorders. *Archives of General Psychiatry, 46,* 776-782.

Kovacs, M., & Goldston, D. (1991). Cognitive and social cognitive development of depressed children and adolescents. *Journal of the American Academy of Child and Adolescent Psychiatry, 30,* 388-392.

Kovacs, M., Obrosky, S., Gatsonis, C., & Richards, C. (1997). First episode major depressive and dysthymic disorder in childhood: Clinical and sociodemographic factors in recovery. *Journal of the American Academy of Child and Adolescent Psychiatry, 36,* 777-784.

Kronenberger, W. M., & Meyer, R. G. (1996). *The Child Clinician's Handbook.* Boston: Allyn & Bacon.

LaFramboise, T. D., & Low, K. G. (1998). American Indian children and adolescents. In J. T. Gibbs & L. N. Huang (Eds.), *Children of Color: Psychological Interventions With Culturally Diverse Youth* (pp. 112-142). San Francisco: Jossey-Bass.

La Greca, A. M. (1997). Children's problems with friends. *In Session: Psychotherapy in Practice, 3,* 21-41.

Last, C. G., & Perrin, S. (1993). Anxiety disorders in African-American and White children. *Journal of Abnormal Child Psychology, 21,* 153-164.

Last, C. G., Perrin, S., Hersen, M., & Kazdin, A. E. (1992). DSM-III-R anxiety disorders in children: Sociodemographic and clinical characteristics. *Journal of the American Academy of Child and Adolescent Psychiatry, 31,* 1070-1076.

Last, C. G., Perrin, S., Hersen, M., & Kazdin, A. E. (1996). A prospective study of childhood anxiety disorders. *Journal of the American Academy of Child and Adolescent Psychiatry, 35,* 1502-1510.

Lee, C. M., & Gotlib, I. H. (1989). Maternal depression and child adjustment: A longitudinal analysis. *Journal of Abnormal Psychology, 98,* 78-85.

Leitenberg, H., Yost, L. W., & Carroll-Wilson, M. (1986). Negative cognitive errors in children: Questionnaire development, normative data, comparisons between children with and without self-reported symptoms of depression, low self-esteem, and evaluation anxiety. *Journal of Consulting and Clinical Psychology, 54,* 528-536.

Lerner, J., Safren, S. A., Henin, A., Warman, M., Heimberg, R. G., & Kendall, P. C. (1999). Differentiating anxious and depressive self-statements in youth: Factor structure of the Negative Affect Self-Statement Questionnaire among youth referred to an anxiety disorders clinic. *Journal of Clinical Child Psychology, 28,* 82-93.

Leve, R. M. (1995). *Child and Adolescent Psychotherapy: Process and Integration.* Boston: Allyn & Bacon.

Malcarne, V. L., & Ingram, R. E. (1994). Cognition and negative affectivity. In T. H. Ollendick & R. J. Prinz (Eds.), *Advances in Clinical Child Psychology* (Vol. 16, pp. 141-176). New York: Plenum.

Manassis, K., & Hood, J. (1998). Individual and familial predictors of impairment in childhood anxiety disorders. *Journal of the American Academy of Child and Adolescent Psychiatry, 37,* 428-434.

Masters, J. C., Burish, T. G., Hollon, S. D., & Rimm, D. C. (1987). *Behavior Therapy: Techniques and Empirical Findings* (2nd ed.). San Diego, CA: Harcourt, Brace, Jovanovich.

Meichenbaum, D. H. (1985). *Stress Inoculation Training.* New York: Pergamon.

Nagata, D. K. (1998). The assessment and treatment of Japanese American children and adolescents. In J. T. Gibbs & L. N. Huang (Eds.), *Children of Color: Psychological Interventions With Culturally Diverse Children* (pp. 215-239). San Francisco: Jossey-Bass.

Neal, A. M., & Knisley, H. (1995). What are African-American children afraid of? Part II: A twelve-month follow-up. *Journal of Anxiety Disorders, 9,* 151-161.

Neal, A. M., Lilly, R. S., & Zakis, S. (1993). What are African-American children afraid of? *Journal of Anxiety Disorders, 7,* 129-139.

Nettles, S. M., & Pleck, J. H. (1994). Risk, resilience, and development: The multiple ecologies of black adolescents in the United States. In R. J. Haggerty, L. R. Sherrod, N. Garmezy, & M. Rutter (Eds.), *Stress and Resilience in Children and Adolescents* (pp. 147-181). New York: Cambridge University Press.

Nolen-Hoeksema, S., & Girgus, J. S. (1995). Explanatory style, achievement, depression, and gender differences in childhood and early adolescence. In G. M. Buchanan & M. E. P. Seligman (Eds.), *Explanatory Style* (pp. 57-70). New York: Lawrence Erlbaum.

Nolen-Hoeksema, S., Girgus, J. S., & Seligman, M. E. P. (1996). Predictors and consequences of childhood depressive symptoms: A five year longitudinal study. *Journal of Abnormal Psychology, 101,* 405-422.

Nolen-Hoeksema, S., Seligman, M. E. P., & Girgus, J. S. (1986). Learned helplessness in children: A longitudinal study of depression, achievement, and explanatory style. *Journal of Personality and Social Psychology, 51,* 435-442.

Nolen-Hoeksema, S., Wolfson, A., Mumme, D., & Guskin, K. (1995). Helplessness in children of depression and nondepressed mothers. *Developmental Psychology, 31,* 377-387.

Oakley, M. E., & Padesky, C. A. (1990). Cognitive therapy for anxiety disorders. In M. Hersen, R. M. Eisler, & P. M. Miller (Eds.), *Progress in Behavior Modification* (pp. 11-45). Newbury Park, CA: Sage.

Ollendick, T. H., & King, N. J. (1998). Empirically supported treatments for children with phobic and anxiety disorders: Current status. *Journal of Clinical Child Psychology, 27,* 156-167.

Ollendick, T. H., & Ollendick, D. G. (1997). General worry and anxiety in children. *In Session: Psychotherapy in Practice, 3,* 89-102.

Padesky, C. A. (1986, September). *Cognitive Therapy Approaches for Treating Depression and Anxiety in Children.* Paper presented at the 2nd International Conference on Cognitive Psychotherapy, Umea, Sweden.

Padesky, C. A. (1988). *Intensive Training Series in Cognitive Therapy* (10-month workshop series). Newport Beach, CA.

Patterson, G. R. (1976). *Living With Children: New Methods for Parents and Teachers.* Champaign, IL: Research Press.

Pedersen, P. (1994). *Handbook of Multicultural Awareness* (2nd ed.). Alexandria, VA: American Counseling Association.

Perrin, S., & Last, C. G. (1997). Worrisome thoughts in children clinically referred for anxiety disorder. *Journal of Clinical Child Psychology, 26,* 181-189.

Persons, J. B. (1989). *Cognitive Therapy in Practice.* New York: W.W. Norton.

Peterson, C., & Seligman, M. E. P. (1984). Causal explanations as a risk factor for depression. *Psychological Review, 91,* 347-374.

Pinderhughes, E. (1989). *Understanding Race, Ethnicity, and Power.* New York: The Free Press.

Politano, P., Nelson, W., Evans, H., Sorenson, S., & Zeman, D. (1986). Factor analytic evaluation of differences between Black and Caucasian emotionally disturbed children on the Children's Depression Inventory. *Journal of Psychopathology and Behavioral Assessment, 8,* 1-7.

Pollock, R. A., Rosenbaum, J. F., Marrs, A., Miller, B. S., & Biederman, J. (1995). Anxiety disorders of childhood: Implications for adult psychopathology. *Psychiatric Clinics of North America, 18,* 745-766.

Polyson, J., & Kimball, W. (1993). Social skills training with physically aggressive children. In A. J. Finch, W. M. Nelson, & E. S. Ott (Eds.), *Cognitive-Behavioral Procedures With Children and Adolescents: A Practical Guide* (pp. 206-232). Boston: Allyn & Bacon.

Quiggle, N. L., Garber, J., Panak, W. F., & Dodge, K. A. (1992). Social information processing in aggressive and depressed children. *Child Development, 63,* 1305-1320.

Ramirez, O. (1998). Mexican American children and adolescents. In J. T. Gibbs & L. N. Huang (Eds.), *Children of Color: Psychological Interventions With Culturally Diverse Youth* (pp. 215-239). San Francisco: Jossey-Bass.

Reynolds, C. R., & Richmond, B. O. (1985). *Revised Children's Manifest Anxiety Scale*. Los Angeles: Western Psychological Services.

Riskind, J. H. (1991). A set of cognitive priming interventions for cognitive therapy homework exercises. *The Behavior Therapist, 14,* 43.

Riskind, J. H., Sarampote, C. S., & Mercier, M. A. (1996). For every malady a sovereign cure: Optimism training. *Journal of Cognitive Psychotherapy, 10,* 105-118.

Robins, C. J., & Hayes, A. M. (1993). An appraisal of cognitive therapy. *Journal of Consulting and Clinical Psychology, 61,* 205-214.

Ronen, T. (1997). *Cognitive Developmental Therapy for Children.* New York: John Wiley.

Ronen, T. (1998). Linking developmental and emotional elements into child and family cognitive-behavioral therapy. In P. Graham (Ed.), *Cognitive-Behaviour Therapy for Children and Families* (pp. 1-17). Cambridge, UK: Cambridge University Press.

Rotter, J. B. (1982). *The Development of Social Learning Theory.* New York: Praeger.

Rudolph, K. D., Hammen, C., & Burge, D. (1997). A cognitive-interpersonal approach to depressive symptoms in preadolescent children. *Journal of Abnormal Child Psychology, 25,* 33-45.

Rutter, J. G., & Friedberg, R. D. (1999). Guidelines for the effective use of socratic dialogue in cognitive therapy. In L. VandeCreek, S. Knapp, & T. L. Jackson (Eds.), *Innovations in Clinical Practice: A Source Book* (Vol. 17, pp. 481-490). Sarasota, FL: Professional Resource Press.

Ryan, N. D., Puig-Antich, J., Ambrosini, P., Rabinovich, H., Robinson, D., Nelson, B., Iyenar, S., & Twomey, J. (1987). The clinical picture of major depression in children and adolescents. *Archives of General Psychiatry, 44,* 854-861.

Sanders, D. E., Merrell, K. W., & Cobb, H. C. (1999). Internalizing symptoms and affect of children with emotional disorders: A comparative study with an urban African-American sample. *Psychology in the Schools, 36,* 187-197.

Schaeffer, C. E., & Millman, H. L. (1981). *How to Help Children With Common Problems.* New York: Signet.

Schwartz, J. A. J., Gladstone, T. R. G., & Kaslow, N. J. (1998). Depressive disorders. In T. H. Ollendick & M. Hersen (Eds.), *Handbook of Child Psychopathology* (3rd ed., pp. 269-289). New York: Plenum.

Seligman, M. E. P., Reivich, K., Jaycox, L., & Gillham, J. E. (1995). *The Optimistic Child.* Boston: Houghton & Mifflin.

Silverman, W. K., & Ginsburg, G. S. (1995). Specific phobia and generalized anxiety disorder. In J. S. March (Ed.), *Anxiety Disorders in Children and Adolescents* (pp. 151-180). New York: Guilford.

Silverman, W. K., & Ginsburg, G. S. (1998). Anxiety disorders. In T. H. Ollendick & M. Hersen (Eds.), *Handbook of Child Psychopathology* (3rd ed., pp. 239-268). New York: Plenum.

Silverman, W. K., Ginsburg, G. S., & Kurtines, W. M. (1995). Clinical issues in treating children with anxiety and phobic disorders. *Cognitive and Behavioral Practice, 2,* 93-117.

Silverman, W. K., & Kurtines, W. M. (1996). *Anxiety and Phobic Disorders: A Pragmatic Approach.* New York: Plenum.

Silverman, W. K., La Greca, A. M., & Wasserstein, S. (1995). What do children worry about? Worries and their relation to anxiety. *Child Development, 66,* 671-686.

Speier, P. L., Sherak, D. L., Hirsch, S., & Cantwell, D. (1995). Depression in children and adolescents. In E. E. Beckham (Ed.), *Handbook of Depression* (pp. 467-525). New York: Guilford.

Spiegler, M. D., & Guevremont, D. C. (1995). *Contemporary Behavior Therapy.* Pacific Grove, CA: Brooks/Cole.

Spivack, G., Platt, J. J., & Shure, M. B. (1976). *The Problem-Solving Approach to Adjustment.* San Francisco: Jossey-Bass.

Spivack, G., & Shure, M. B. (1982). The cognition of social adjustment: Interpersonal cognitive problem-solving training. In B. B. Lahey & A. E. Kazdin (Eds.), *Advances in Clinical Child Psychology* (Vol. 5, pp. 323-372). New York: Plenum.

Stark, K. D. (1990). *Childhood Depression: School-Based Intervention.* New York: Guilford.

Stark, K. D., Rouse, L. W., & Livingstone, R. (1991). Treatment of depression during childhood and adolescence: Cognitive-behavior procedures for individual and family. In P. C. Kendall (Ed.), *Child and Adolescent Therapy: Cognitive-Behavior Procedures* (pp. 165-206). New York: Guilford.

Stark, K. D., Swearer, S., Kurowski, C., Sommer, D., & Bowen, B. (1996). Targeting the child and the family: A holistic approach to treating child and adolescent depressive disorders. In E. D. Hibbs & P. S. Jensen (Eds.), *Psychosocial Treatments for Child and Adolescent Disorders: Empirically-Based Strategies for Clinical Practice* (pp. 207-238). Washington, DC: American Psychological Association.

Strauss, C. C., Lease, C. A., Last, C. G., & Francis, G. (1988). Overanxious disorder: An examination of developmental differences. *Journal of Abnormal Child Psychology, 16,* 433-443.

Thompson, M., Kaslow, N. J., Weiss, B., & Nolen-Hoeksema, S. (1998). Children's Attributional Style Questionnaire-Revised. *Psychological Assessment, 10,* 166-190.

Treadwell, K. R. H., Flannery-Schroeder, E. C., & Kendall, P. C. (1995). Ethnicity and gender in relation to adaptive functioning, diagnostic status, and treatment outcome in children from an anxiety clinic. *Journal of Anxiety Disorders, 9,* 373-384.

Turner, J. E., & Cole, D. A. (1994). Developmental differences in cognitive diatheses for child depression. *Journal of Abnormal Psychology, 22,* 15-32.

Vasey, M. W. (1993). Development and cognition in childhood anxiety. In T. H. Ollendick & R. J. Prinz (Eds.), *Advances in Clinical Child Psychology* (Vol. 15, pp. 1-39). New York: Plenum.

Vasey, M. W., Crnic, K., & Carter, W. G. (1994). Worry in childhood: A developmental perspective. *Cognitive Therapy and Research, 18,* 529-549.

Vernon, A. (1989). *Thinking, Feeling, and Behaving: An Emotional Educational Curriculum for Children.* Champaign, IL: Research Press.

Vernon, A. (1998). *The Passport Program: A Journey Through Emotional, Social, Cognitive, and Self-Development.* Chicago, IL: Research Press.

Vernon, A., & Al-Mabuk, R. H. (1995). *What Growing Up Is All About: A Parent's Guide to Child and Adolescent Development.* Champaign, IL: Research Press.

Waxman, R. P., Weist, M. D., & Benson, D. M. (1999). Toward collaboration in the growing education-mental health interface. *Clinical Psychology Review, 19,* 239-253.

Weems, C. F., Hammond-Laurence, K., Silverman, W. K., & Ferguson, C. (1997). The relationship between anxiety sensitivity and depression in children and adolescents referred for anxiety. *Behavior Research and Therapy, 35,* 961-966.

Weems, C. F., Hammond-Laurence, K., Silverman, W. K., & Ginsburg, G. S. (1998). Testing the utility of the anxiety sensitivity construct in children and adolescents referred for anxiety disorders. *Journal of Clinical Child Psychology, 27,* 69-77.

Weist, M. D. (1997). Expanded school mental health services: A national movement in progress. In T. H. Ollendick & R. J. Prinz (Eds.), *Advances in Clinical Child Psychology* (Vol. 19, pp. 319-352). New York: Plenum.

Weisz, J. R., Huey, S. J., & Weersing, V. R. (1998). Psychotherapy outcome research with children and adolescents. In T. H. Ollendick & R. J. Prinz (Eds.), *Advances in Clinical Child Psychology* (Vol. 20, pp. 49-91). New York: Plenum.

Weisz, J. R., Sweeney, L., Profitt, V., & Carr, T. (1992). Control-related beliefs and self-reported depressive symptoms in late childhood. *Journal of Abnormal Psychology, 102,* 411-418.

Yung, B., & Hammond, R. W. (1995). *Positive Adolescent Choices Training (PACT): A Model for Violence Prevention Groups With African-American Youth-Program Guide.* Champaign, IL: Research Press.

# Subject Index

## A

Acuity of problems, 11
African-American youth, 18-21
Agenda setting, 3, 26, 33-35, 70, 77
Anxiety sensitivity, 46-47
Asian-American youth, 22-23

## B

Balance between structure and process, 38-40
Behavioral inhibition, 46-47

## C

Cognitive model, 2
Collaborative empiricism, 3, 26, 31-33
Chronological age, 11
Comorbidity issues with anxious and depressed youth, 8-10
Cognitive characteristics
    anxious children, 51-52
    depressed children, 62-63
Culturally responsive intervention, 26

**L**

Language, 27

**N**

Native-American youth, 21-22
Noncompliance with homework, anxious children, 57

**P**

PANDY Program, 2, 10, 43, 77, 78, 90-91, 99, 103
Parental overprotection of anxious children, 58, 88-89
Parental variables and childhood anxiety and depression, 85-88
Parents' emotional perfectionism, 89-90
Perfectionistic children, 71-72
Providing feedback to parents, 90-91, 101-102

**R**

Reading level, 11-12

**S**

School-based groups, 94-96
Seamless integration of exercises into therapy, 37-38
Session structure, 33, 77
Skill acquisition versus skill application, 41-42
Strategies for pessimistic children, 65, 70
Symptoms of
        Depression, 61-62
        Generalized Anxiety Disorder, 48-49
        Social Anxiety, 49-51

**T**

Therapist overprotection of anxious children, 58
Thought testing,
        anxious children, 54-55
        depressed children, 68-69

**W**

Working with parents, 88-90
Worries, 45-46

# If You Found This Book Useful . . .

You might want to know more about our other titles.

If you would like to receive our latest catalog, please return this form:

Name: _____
(Please Print)

Address: _____

Address: _____

City/State/Zip: _____
This is ☐ home ☐ office

Telephone: (_____)_____

I am a:

☐ Psychologist
☐ Psychiatrist
☐ School Psychologist
☐ Clinical Social Worker

☐ Mental Health Counselor
☐ Marriage and Family Therapist
☐ Not in Mental Health Field
☐ Other: _____

◆　　　　　◆　　　　　◆

**Professional Resource Press
P.O. Box 15560
Sarasota, FL 34277-1560**

**Telephone: 800-443-3364
FAX: 941-343-9201
E-mail: mail@prpress.com
Website: http://www.prpress.com**